Organic Chemistry
Science Fair Projects

Library of Congress Cataloging-in-Publication Data

Gardner, Robert, 1929–
 Organic chemistry science fair projects, revised and expanded using the scientific method /
by Robert Gardner and Barbara Gardner Conklin.
     p. cm. — (Chemistry science projects using the scientific method)
 Summary: "Explains how to use the scientific method to conduct several science experiments with
organic chemistry. Includes ideas for science fair projects"—Provided by publisher.
 Includes bibliographical references and index.
 ISBN 978-0-7660-3414-3
 1. Chemistry, Organic—Experiments—Juvenile literature. 2. Science projects—Juvenile literature.
I. Conklin, Barbara Gardner. II. Title.
 QD257.5.G369 2010
 547.0078—dc22
                            2008050078

Printed in the United States of America

092009 Lake Book Manufacturing, Inc., Melrose Park, IL

10 9 8 7 6 5 4 3 2 1

To Our Readers: We have done our best to make sure all Internet Addresses in this book
were active and appropriate when we went to press. However, the author and the publisher
have no control over and assume no liability for the material available on those Internet sites
or on other Web sites they may link to. Any comments or suggestions can be sent by e-mail
to comments@enslow.com or to the address on the back cover.

♻ Enslow Publishers, Inc. is committed to printing our books on recycled paper. The paper in
every book contains between 10% to 30% post-consumer waste (PCW). The cover board on the
outside of each book contains 100% PCW. Our goal is to do our part to help young people and
the environment too!

Illustration Credits: Tom LaBaff and Stephanie LaBaff

Editorial Revision: Lily Book Productions

Design: Oxygen Design

Photo Credits: Crecart/iStockphoto.com, p. 138; Emrah Turudu/iStockphoto.com, p. 116;
Joeri van Veen/iStockphoto.com, p. 28; Katharina Wittfeld/iStockphoto.com, p. 6;
Matteu Rinaldi/iStockphoto.com, p. 74; Shutterstock, pp. 3, 48.

Cover Photos: Joeri van Veen/iStockphoto.com (onion); Katharina Wittfeld/iStockphoto.com (hands with grain);
Matteu Rinaldi/iStockphoto.com (molecule models); Shutterstock (bubbles, diamond, gumdrops, soap).

Revised Edition of *Chemistry Science Fair Projects Using French Fries, Gumdrops, Soap, and
Other Organic Stuff.* Copyright © 2004.

Science Projects
cientific Method

Organic Chemistry Science Fair Projects

Revised and Expanded
Using the Scientific Method

Robert Gardner and
Barbara Gardner Conklin

Enslow Publishers, Inc.
40 Industrial Road
Box 398
Berkeley Heights, NJ 07922
USA

http://www.enslow.com

Contents

Indicates experiments that contain Science Project Ideas.

INTRODUCTION

Organic Chemistry Experiments and Projects Using the Scientific Method

Chemistry is the part of science that deals with what materials are made of and how they combine with one another. Organic chemistry, the subject of this book, studies all the millions of compounds that contain carbon. Another book in this series deals with inorganic chemistry, substances lacking carbon.

Since foods are made up of organic compounds, part of this book involves experiments on foods and cooking. In doing those experiments, you'll be spending

◀ Carbon is found in every living thing, from grains like wheat to the humans that cultivate it.

a lot of time in your kitchen laboratory making use of the stove, refrigerator, and sink. But to give you a sense of what carbon compounds are like, we'll first explore their properties. Chapters 1 through 3 will explain why chemicals change. They'll help you understand what happens in your kitchen experiments.

This book contains lots of fun experiments about organic chemistry. You'll also be given suggestions for independent investigations that you can do yourself. Many of the experiments are followed by a section called Science Project Ideas. This section contains great ideas for your own science fair projects.

The experiments are all easy to do and safe to carry out when the instructions are followed as given. Consult with your school science teacher or some other responsible adult to obtain approval before starting any experiments of your own.

If any danger is involved in doing an experiment, it will be made known to you. In some cases, to avoid any danger to you, you'll be asked to work with an adult. Please do so. We don't want you to take any chances that could lead to an injury.

Most of the materials you'll need to carry out the projects and experiments described in this book can be found in your home. Several of the experiments may require items that you can buy from a supermarket, a hobby or toy shop, a hardware store, or one of the science supply companies listed in the appendix. As you begin to use this book, show it to one of the science teachers in your school. Perhaps the teacher will allow you and some of your friends to use the school's equipment. At times, you'll need a partner to help you. It would be best if you work with friends or adults who enjoy experimenting as much as you do. In that way you'll both enjoy what you're doing.

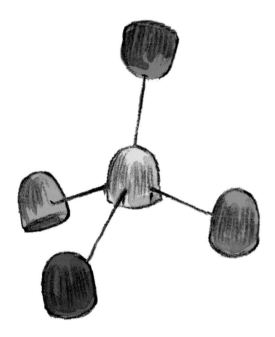

How Scientists
Search for Answers

When scientists have a question to answer, they start by researching. They read scientific literature and consult online science databases that are maintained by universities, research centers, or the government. There, they can study abstracts—summaries of reports—by scientists who have conducted experiments or done similar research in the field.

In this way, they find out whether other scientists have examined the same question or have tried to answer it by doing an experiment. Careful research will tell what kind of experiments, if any, have been done to try to answer the question.

Scientists don't want to repeat experiments that have known and accepted outcomes. Also, they want to avoid repeating any mistakes others may have made while doing similar experiments. If no one else has done scientific work that answers the question, scientists then do further research on how best to do the experiment.

While researching for the experiment, the scientist tries to guess—or predict—the possible results. This prediction is called a hypothesis.

The scientist hopes that a well-researched and carefully planned experiment will prove the hypothesis to be true. At times, however, the results of even the best-planned experiment can be far different from what the scientist expected. Yet even if the results indicate the hypothesis was not true, this does not mean the experiment was a failure. In fact, unexpected results can provide valuable information that leads to a different answer or to another, even better, experiment.

Using the Scientific Method in Experiments and Projects

The Scientific Method

A scientific experiment starts when someone wonders what would happen if certain conditions were set up and tested by following a specific process. For example, in an experiment testing the ability of table salt (sodium chloride) to conduct electricity, you can ask the question: "Is table salt more conductive when it is dissolved in water to make a saltwater solution?" To find the answer, some possible guesses, hypotheses, would be:

✓ Solid table salt conducts electricity better than salt water.

✓ Salt water conducts electricity better than solid table salt.

✓ Neither form of table salt will conduct electricity.

Let's say your hypothesis is that salt water will conduct electricity better than the solid table salt. For a start, we have to know that a scientific experiment can have only two variables—that is, only two things that can change. For this experiment, one variable is whether the salt is dissolved in water or whether it is solid. The other variable will be the electrical conductivity of each form of salt.

The form of salt is allowed to change (either a solid or in solution) but not the equipment producing the electrical charge, and not the amount or strength of the charge the equipment produces. If the electrical charge differed when the solid salt and the salt solution were tested, then we couldn't tell how the conductivity of one form compared to the other.

Now, if the experiment is carried out and the results show there is no difference in the conductivity of solid salt and dissolved salt, this would not mean your experiment is a failure. Even if your hypothesis—dissolved salt conducts electricity better—turns out to be false, the results of your experiment still can provide important information. And these results may lead to further ideas that can be explored.

Scientists may develop logical explanations for the results of their experiments. These explanations, or theories, then must be tested by more experiments. If the resulting data from more experiments provide compelling support for a theory, then that theory could be accepted by the world of science. But scientists are careful about accepting new theories. If the resulting data contradict a theory, then the theory must be discarded, altered, or retested. That is the scientific method.

Basic Steps in the Scientific Method

The best experiments and science projects usually follow the scientific method's basic steps:

✓ Ask questions about what would happen if certain conditions or events were set up and tested in an experiment.

✓ Do background research to investigate the subject of your questions until you have a main question.

✓ Construct a hypothesis—an answer to your question—that you can then test and investigate with an experiment.

✓ Design and conduct an experiment to test your hypothesis.

✓ Keep records, collecting data, and then analyze what you've recorded.

✓ Draw a conclusion based on the experiment and the data you've recorded.

✓ Write a report about your results.

Your Hypothesis

Many experiments and science projects begin by asking whether something can be done or how it can be done. In this book's experiment, "Food Coloring, Water, Milk, and Soap," the question is: "Does food coloring made from water and alcohol behave the same way when it is added to water or to milk?"

How do you search for an answer? For your hypothesis? First, you should study the chemical nature of milk, water, alcohol, and soap. You'll learn about the solubility of liquid fats when they're mixed with water and alcohol. And you'll find out something special about the molecular makeup of soap: its polarity. Soap's polarity makes it so effective in this experiment.

After your research, you might make an educated guess in answer to the question; this is your hypothesis: "No, food coloring is soluble in water, but not in milk." You'll also find out what methods, materials, and equipment are needed to design an experiment that tests your hypothesis. You'll find the right tools and materials—in this case samples of the milk, a plastic cup, a cotton swab, and a kitchen table or counter.

Remember: To give your experiment or project every chance of success, prepare a hypothesis that is clear and brief. The simpler the better.

Designing the Experiment

Your experiment will be structured to investigate whether the hypothesis is true or false. The experiment is intended to test the hypothesis, not necessarily to prove that the hypothesis is right.

The results of a well-designed experiment are more valuable than the results of an experiment that is intentionally designed to give the answer you want. The conditions you set up in your experiment must be a fair test of your hypothesis. For example, in the conductivity of table salt experiment you should follow the instructions carefully when sending the electric charge into the solid salt and the salt solution. Each should receive the same amount of electricity, and then you'll know that your results are accurate.

By carefully carrying out your experiment you'll discover useful information that can be recorded as data (observations). It's most important that the experiment's procedures and results are as accurate as possible. Design the experiment for observable, measurable results. And keep it simple, because the more complicated your experiment is, the more chance you have for error.

Also, if you have friends helping you with an experiment or project, make sure from the start that they'll take their tasks seriously.

Remember: Scientists around the world always use metric measurements in their experiments and projects, and so should you. Use metric liquid and dry measures and a Celsius thermometer.

Recording Data

Your hypothesis, procedure, data, and conclusions should be recorded immediately as you experiment, but don't keep it on loose scraps of paper. Record your data in a notebook or log-book—one you use just for experiments. Your notebook should be bound so that you have a permanent record. The laboratory notebook is an essential part of all academic and scientific research.

Make sure to include the date, experiment number, and a brief description of how you collected the data. Write clearly. If you have to cross something out, do it with just a single line, then rewrite the correct information.

Repeat your experiment several times to be sure your results are consistent and your data are trustworthy. Don't try to interpret data as you go along. It's better first to record results accurately, then study them later.

You might even find that you want to replace your experiment's original question with a new one. For example, by answering the question, "What is the chemical process behind yeast as a leavening agent?" you learn that yeast consumes sugar (glucose). This brings up other questions: "Is there a limit to how much sugar yeast can digest? Can too much sugar inhibit the leavening process?"

Writing the Science Fair Report

Communicate the results of your experiment by writing a clear report. Even the most successful experiment loses its value if the scientist cannot clearly tell what happened. Your report should describe how the experiment was designed and conducted and should state its precise results.

Following are the parts of a science fair report, in the order they should appear:

• The Title Page

The title of your experiment should be centered and near the top of the page. Your teacher will tell you what other information is needed, such as your name, grade, and the name of your science teacher.

• Table of Contents

On the report's second page, list the remaining parts of the report and their page numbers.

• Abstract

Give a brief overview of your experiment. In just a few sentences, tell the purpose of the experiment, what you did, and what you found out. Always write in plain, clear language.

• Introduction

State your hypothesis and explain how you came up with it. Discuss your experiment's main question and how your research led to the hypothesis. Tell what you hoped to achieve when you started the experiment.

• Experiment and Data

This is a detailed step-by-step explanation of how you organized and carried out the experiment. Explain what methods you followed and what materials and equipment you used.

State when the experiment was done (the date and perhaps the time of day) and under what conditions (in a laboratory, outside on a windy day, in cold or warm weather, etc.). Tell who was involved and what part they played in the experiment.

Include clearly labeled graphs and tables of data from the experiment as well as any photographs or drawings that help illustrate your work. Anyone who reads your report should be able to repeat the experiment just the way you did it. (Repeating an experiment is a good way to test whether the original results were obtained correctly.)

• Discussion

Explain your results and conclusions, perhaps comparing them with published scientific data you first read about in your research. Consider how the experiment's results relate to your hypothesis. Ask yourself: Do my results support or contradict my hypothesis? Then analyze the answer.

Would you do anything differently if you did this experiment again? State what you've learned as a result of the experiment.

Analyze how your tools and equipment did their tasks, and how well you and others used those tools. If you think the experiment could be done better if designed another way or if you have another hypothesis that might be tested, then include this in your discussion.

• Conclusion

Make a brief summary of your experiment's results. Include only information and data already stated in the report, and be sure not to bring in any new information.

• Acknowledgments

Give credit to everyone who helped you with the experiment. State the names of these individuals and briefly explain who they are and how they assisted you.

• References / Bibliography

List any books, magazines, journals, articles, Web sites, scientific databases, and interviews that were important to your research for the experiment.

Science Fairs

Science fair judges tend to reward creative thought and imagination. It's difficult to be creative or imaginative unless you're really interested in your project. So, be sure to choose a subject that appeals to you. And before you jump into a project, consider your own talents and the cost of materials you'll need.

Remember, judges at science fairs don't reward projects or experiments that are simply copied from a book. For example, a diagram or model of an atom or molecule wouldn't impress most judges. However, you would attract their attention by designing an experiment to show how everyday cooking and baking uses organic chemistry involving carbon compounds, acids, and chemical reactions.

If you decide to use a project from this book for a science fair, you should find ways to modify or extend it. This shouldn't be difficult because you'll probably discover that, as you do these projects, new ideas for experiments will come to mind. These experiments could make excellent science fair projects, particularly because the ideas are your own and are interesting to you.

If you decide to enter a science fair and have never done so before, you should read some of the books listed in the Further Reading section and visit the Internet sites. The books and sites with titles that refer to science fairs will provide plenty of helpful hints and information that will help you avoid the pitfalls that sometimes plague first-time entrants. You'll learn how to prepare appealing reports that include charts and graphs, how to set up and display your work, how to present your project, and how to relate to judges and visitors.

Following are some suggestions to consider.

Some Tips for Success at a Science Fair

Science teachers and science fair judges have many different opinions on what makes a good science fair project or experiment. Here are the most important elements:

Originality of Concept is one of the most important things judges consider. Some judges believe that the best science fair projects answer a question that is not found in a science textbook.

Scientific Content is another main area of evaluation. How was science applied in the procedure? Are there sufficient data? Did you stick to your intended procedure and keep good records?

Thoroughness is next in importance. Was the experiment repeated as often as needed to test your hypothesis? Is your notebook complete, and are the data accurate? Does your research bibliography show you did enough library work?

Clarity in how you present your exhibit shows you had a good understanding of the subject you worked on. It's important that your exhibit clearly presents the results of your work.

Effective Process: Judges recognize that how skillfully you carry out a science fair project is usually more important than its results. A well-done project gives students the best understanding of what scientists actually do day-to-day.

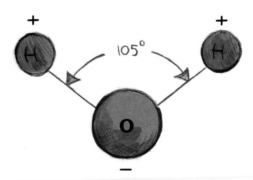

Other points to consider when preparing for your science fair:

The Abstract: Write up a brief explanation of your project and make copies for visitors or judges who want to read it.

Knowledge: Be ready to answer questions from visitors and judges confidently. Know what is in your notebook and make some notes on index cards to remind you of important points.

Practice: Before the science fair begins, prepare a list of several questions you think you might be asked. Think about the answers and about how your display can help to support them. Have a friend or parent ask you questions and answer them out loud. Knowing your work thoroughly helps you feel more confident when you're asked about it.

Appearance: Dress and act in a way that shows you take your project seriously. Visitors and judges should get the impression that you're interested in the project and take pride in answering their questions about it.

Remember: Don't block your exhibit. Stand to the side when someone is looking at it.

Projects about chemistry have special needs with respect to displays. You cannot show the chemical changes as they take place. Instead, photograph or draw them. Many chemical changes are colorful, so use color to make pictures more striking. Show the materials used at the start of the reaction and those produced at the end of the reaction by enclosing them in containers such as sealed petri dishes or plastic bags that you mount on a display. Photograph or draw any special laboratory tools and the laboratory apparatus you set up. Be inventive about different ways of showing what took place.

Safety First

Most of the projects included in this book are perfectly safe, but it's your responsibility to do them only as directed. Experimenting with chemicals can be dangerous unless certain precautions are taken. The precautions necessary to prevent accidents and to make the experiments safe and enjoyable are easy to follow.

✔ Consideration must always be given to safety. Therefore, it's essential that **all investigations and science fair projects be approved by a responsible adult.** Where warranted, the experimentation should take place under adult supervision. If there are any questions about safety, the adult should be sure to obtain the approval of a science teacher before allowing the experiments.

✔ Whenever doing chemistry experiments, **wear goggles** (safety glasses). All chemists wear goggles when working in the laboratory. Goggles can be purchased in hardware or dollar stores. Most of the substances are not dangerous, but they might sting your eyes if they splatter.

✔ Read all instructions carefully before proceeding with a project. If you have questions, check with your supervisor before going any further.

✔ Never taste any materials listed in this book unless specifically directed to do so. Never put your fingers to your mouth while working on an experiment.

✔ Always wash your hands with warm water and soap after an experiment. Also, wash the surfaces on which you have carried out the experiment.

✔ Never use a mercury thermometer because exposure to mercury is dangerous; use mercury-free alternatives, such as thermometers containing alcohol.

✔ When using certain solvents, adequate ventilation is necessary, such as an exhaust fan or an open window.

✔ Never heat liquid organic compounds such as alcohol over an open flame.

✔ Wear plastic gloves when handling chemicals. The thin disposable gloves that may be used on either hand and are sold in packs of one hundred in dollar stores or hardware stores are very convenient for this purpose.

✔ Some chemicals should not be flushed down the sink or thrown into the garbage. Instructions will be given for disposal of any such materials used in an experiment.

✔ Maintain a serious attitude while conducting experiments. Fooling around can be dangerous to you and to others.

✔ Never let water droplets come in contact with a hot light bulb.

✔ Never experiment with household electricity except under the supervision of **a knowledgeable adult.**

✔ It's a good idea to wear an apron and to work on surfaces that can resist water damage. Covering a surface with newspapers or plastic sheeting will help to protect it.

✔ You should use purified water for experiments unless otherwise stated. Distilled or deionized water sold at the supermarket may be used for this purpose. Natural water from a spring or other source may be safe to drink but is not considered pure because it contains dissolved solids.

And now, on to the experiments!

CHAPTER 1

Organic Chemistry in Your Life

Organic chemistry is about all materials that contain carbon. As you cook, eat, and digest food, organic chemistry is at work. When you do the laundry or dishes, organic chemicals are used. You're surrounded by organic chemicals and their reactions every day of your life. But some chemical actions and reactions are more evident than others.

A chemical reaction is a process in which one or more substances change to form new substances. The new substances have different properties than the original ones. In the process energy is usually absorbed or released.

◄ Cutting an onion breaks its cell walls and releases a gas that comes into contact with water in our eyes. This forms a sulfuric acid solution that can sting our eyes.

How do you know if a chemical reaction has occurred? Signs of a chemical reaction include a color change, a temperature change, a new odor, gas bubbles, a precipitate (a new solid that is formed), burning, or explosions. Toasted bread, for example, is the result of a chemical reaction. It's bread that has been slightly burned on each side. You can see a color change and feel a texture change in the bread. The heat from the toaster causes changes in the starches, sugars, and proteins on the bread's surface. If you leave the bread in the toaster for too long, it turns black. This suggests that chemicals in the bread have been broken down into carbon and other products.

Scientists work with chemicals by studying their qualities. In this chapter you'll begin exploring the color of materials, whether those materials are strong or bland, and whether they form crystals. There are many clues scientists use to identify chemicals and to understand how they mix and work together.

Elements and Compounds

Scientists in the 1600s learned through their experiments that almost all matter such as rocks, soil, and seawater is made up of mixtures. These mixtures can be separated into "pure" substances whose qualities (density, solubility, boiling temperature, etc.) don't change. Pure substances are of two types: elements and compounds.

Elements cannot be broken down further without losing their qualities. Compounds, on the other hand, contain two or more elements. Scientists have discovered more than a hundred elements. Carbon is one of the most abundant elements in nature, as are hydrogen and oxygen. Carbon is found in every living thing, while hydrogen and oxygen together make up water, a compound.

The smallest particle of an element is an atom, and the smallest particle of a compound is a molecule. A molecule contains atoms of the elements that combine to form the compound. For example, a molecule of water (H_2O) is made up of two atoms of hydrogen (H_2) and one atom of oxygen (O).

EXPERIMENT 1.1

Chromatography

Question:

How can organic compounds be separated from their mixtures?

Hypothesis:

Water can separate water-soluble organic compounds, which usually differ in color.

Materials:

- white coffee filter
- tall clear glasses
- water
- scissors
- tape
- colored non-permanent marking pens
- pencils or chopsticks

Chromatography is a method used to separate compounds in a mixture. *Chroma* is the Greek word for "color."

Procedure:

1. Cut a white coffee filter into even strips. You'll need as many strips as you have colored marking pens.

2. On each strip put a dot of just one color about an inch from the bottom. One strip might have a red dot, another a black dot, and so on.

3. Put each strip in a clear tall drinking glass that contains a small amount of water.

4. Tape the strip to a pencil or chopstick so that when the strip is hanging in the glass, the lower edge of the strip is in the water but the colored dot is not (see Figure 1). What happens to the colored dot as water climbs up the filter-paper strip?

Figure 1.

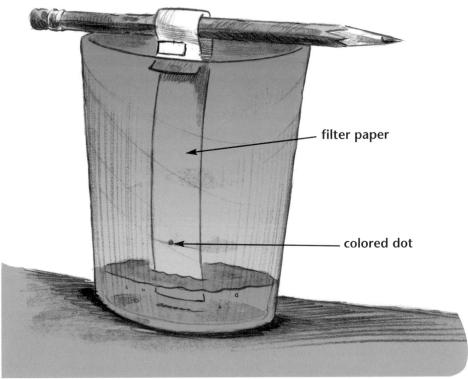

filter paper

colored dot

Chromatography is often used to separate organic compounds.

Results and Conclusions

As the water rises through the paper, it carries compounds in the colored dot with it. The different chemical compounds in the marking pen travel different distances. This separates the compounds on the paper.

Chromatography works because different compounds have different physical properties, such as the weight of their molecules and the forces of attraction between their molecules.

 Science Project Ideas

- Why can't you use permanent markers in this experiment? Try some to find out.

- What could you use in place of water for substances that aren't water soluble (they don't dissolve in water)?

- Can you think of a way to do this experiment with dyed food items such as colored candies?

- Will the temperature of the air or water have any effect on chromatography? What would happen if you used cold water and put the glasses in the refrigerator? How about hot water in a very warm place?

- Examine a piece of filter paper under a microscope. How does the appearance of the paper help you understand why water climbs up the strip?

EXPERIMENT 1.2

Testing for Acids and Bases

Question:

How can you easily identify acids and bases in everyday substances?

Hypothesis:

You can use the juice of plants, such as red cabbage, to identify acids and bases.

Materials:

- **an adult**
- pot
- red cabbage
- water
- stove
- jar
- strainer
- eyedropper
- clear glass

- baking soda
- salt
- sugar
- vinegar
- lemon juice
- household ammonia solution
- cream of tartar
- other household items

Acids and bases have different properties. Acids taste sour and react with some metals to form hydrogen gas. Bases taste bitter and are slippery. Think about how sour a lemon tastes. Lemons are acidic. Think about how hard it is to hold on to soap in the shower. Soap is an example of a base.

The pH scale is a way to measure the strength of an acidic or basic solution. A neutral solution, such as pure water, has a pH of 7. Acids have a pH of 0 to 7, and bases have a pH of 7 to 14. A strong acid has a pH of 0 to 4; a strong base has a pH of 10 to 14. Many of the liquids we deal with in everyday life are weak acids (pH 4–7) or weak bases (pH 7–10).

The leaves of red cabbage can allow you to identify acids and bases. Red cabbage has a pigment called anthocyanin. The pigment's color depends on pH. **Safety:** *Be sure* **an adult** *is present to supervise before you begin because you will be using a stove.*

You can make some red cabbage indicator.

Procedure:

1. Put some red cabbage leaves into a pot. Add enough water to cover the leaves.

2. Boil the cabbage leaves for about 20 minutes.

3. After the liquid has cooled, strain the colored liquid into a jar. The liquid should be purplish.

4. Put a few drops of your cabbage juice indicator in some clear glasses holding small amounts of household items such as lemon juice, baking soda, vinegar, ammonia solution, cream of tartar, salt, sugar, and other substances you may have selected.

Results and Conclusions

If the substance is an acid, the red cabbage juice indicator will turn a pinkish to red color. A base substance will turn the indicator a blue to green color. The indicator remains unchanged in a neutral solution.

Which substances were acids? Which were bases? Were any neutral?

 Science Project Ideas

- You can write invisible messages with an acid such as lemon juice or a base such as baking soda mixed with water. Use a small watercolor brush or a cotton swab to write a message on paper. Let the message dry completely. Then spray the paper with the cabbage juice indicator. Why does the message become visible?

- Try to find other colored vegetables such as beets, rhubarb, or blueberries that might be used as an indicator. Could any of these serve as indicators?

- If you combine two acids, will the combination be a stronger acid? Use pH indicator strips to find out.

- If you mix a substance that you found was acidic with a substance that was a base, will you always form a neutral solution?

EXPERIMENT 1.3

A Teary Experiment

Question:

Do all onions cause your eyes to tear when you cut them?

Hypothesis:

Some onion varieties are easier on the eyes.

Materials:

- **an adult**
- onions, a variety such as white, red, and yellow
- knives
- cutting boards
- water
- refrigerator
- freezer
- white vinegar
- candle
- matches

As you found in the previous experiment, many household items are acidic.

Procedure:

1. Go to a grocery store and buy different types of onions. They usually come in a variety of colors.

2. Under **adult supervision**, cut up different kinds of onions. Take a break between onions to give your eyes some time to recover from any tearing. Be sure to wash and dry your hands after cutting each onion.

   To avoid contamination, use different knives and cutting boards for each onion, or wash them after each use. Do some onions make you cry more than others? Do some onions have more odor than others when you cut them?

   People use many methods to prevent the crying reaction.

3. Under **adult supervision**, try them to see if any work for you. Use the onion that made you cry the most so that you will be able to best decide if the method is working.

4. One method is to cut the onion under water. Does it matter if it's warm or cold water?

5. Another method is to put the onion in the refrigerator or freezer for 10 to 15 minutes before cutting it. Why might the cold temperature change the reaction?

6. Another approach is to put a little white vinegar on the cutting board. Does that help? From the previous experiment, you learned that vinegar is an acid. Why might an acid stop the reaction?

7. Try cutting the onion with a lighted candle nearby. How might a candle flame affect the reaction?

Results and Conclusions

Do any of the methods to prevent crying work for you? Can you think of another approach that might work?

When you cut into an onion, you break its cell walls and a gas is released. When the gas comes in contact with water in your eyes, a chemical reaction occurs and a dilute sulfuric acid solution is formed. When you cry, it's your body's natural defense against the strong acid. Notice that there is also a strong odor, which can indicate a chemical reaction.

 Science Project Ideas

- Are some people more likely to cry than others when an onion is cut? Get some volunteers and see if some people are more sensitive than others. How will you determine sensitivity?

- Will wearing glasses or safety glasses decrease a person's sensitivity to onions? Design an experiment to find out.

- Can a person build up a resistance to crying while cutting onions?

EXPERIMENT 1.4

Acids, Eggs, and Chalk

Question:
What effect do acids have on calcium carbonate?

Hypothesis:
Adding vinegar to eggshells and chalk will show that acid will react with $CaCO_3$.

Materials:
- 4 clear glass jars with lids
- 2 eggs
- water
- white vinegar
- 2 pieces of chalk

As you saw in the previous experiment, acids can make you cry. What effect can they have on other things? To find out, you can test eggshells and chalk.

The shell of an egg is made of calcium carbonate ($CaCO_3$), and chalk is made from a mineral called limestone, which is also calcium carbonate. Many statues and buildings are made of limestone.

Procedure:

1. Find two clear glass jars.

2. Put an egg in each jar. Be careful not to crack the eggshell.

3. Pour enough water in one of the jars to cover the egg.

4. Cover the other egg with the same amount of vinegar, which is acetic acid.

   Does the egg in the water float? Does the egg in the vinegar float?

5. Follow the same procedure for two pieces of chalk.

6. Put covers or lids on all the jars. Observe the jars over the next 24 hours.

Results and Conclusions

Can you predict what will happen to the eggs and chalk in each jar?

Vinegar is acetic acid. It combines with calcium carbonate (limestone) to produce carbon dioxide, water, and calcium acetate. If you saw bubbles form in the jars, what was the gas?

Does either egg float after some time has passed? If an egg is floating, can you explain why it's floating? What happens if you gently shake the bubbles off the egg?

How does this experiment help you understand why scientists are concerned about the effects of acid rain?

Science Project Ideas

- Try the same experiment with two clean chicken bones, but make observations for a week instead of a day. Check the bones for flexibility each day. What do you observe? What mineral is in bones? How can you explain what you've observed?

- Put aluminum foil in the bottom of a glass jar. Put a small amount of tomato paste on the aluminum foil. Place the jar in the refrigerator and observe it periodically for several weeks. Can you explain what happens?

- Many colas contain phosphoric acid. What happens if you put an egg in such a cola?

- Will other acidic substances such as lemon juice and flavored crystals that contain citric acid have the same effect as vinegar on an egg?

- Design your own experiment to determine how acids can affect natural habitats.

EXPERIMENT 1.5

Growing Crystals

Question:

What causes sugar-water solutions to form sugar crystals?

Hypothesis:

When water saturated with dissolved sugar begins to cool, all the sugar is no longer able to stay dissolved. Therefore it crystallizes.

Materials:

- **an adult**
- measuring cup
- water
- small pot
- sugar
- tablespoon
- wooden spoon
- stove
- pot holder
- clear glass jar such as a mason jar
- string
- pencil or chopstick
- clean paper clip

Safety: *Do this experiment under adult supervision because you will be working with a stove and hot substances.*

When you add sugar to water, the sugar dissolves. There is a limit, though, to how much sugar will dissolve in a fixed amount of water. When no more sugar will dissolve in the water, the solution is said to be saturated. Temperature can change the saturation point. As the temperature of the water increases, so does the amount of sugar that can be dissolved. When a saturated solution cools, there is more sugar in the solution than is normally possible. The solution is then supersaturated. Supersaturated solutions can change. As a result, sugar molecules will begin to crystallize with the slightest disturbance.

Procedure:

1. Pour a cup of water into a small pot.

2. Slowly add sugar to the water, one tablespoon at a time. Continuously stir the solution while adding the sugar.

3. Once the solution is saturated (no more sugar will dissolve in the water), heat the solution over medium heat for a few minutes. Any sugar that hadn't dissolved before will dissolve as the temperature rises.

4. Turn off the heat and stir in as much sugar as will dissolve (about two cups).

5. Reheat the sugar water and boil the solution for about a minute. The solution should be clear at this point.

6. Turn off the heat and **ask the adult** to pour the solution into a clear jar.

7. Tie one end of a string to a pencil or chopstick. Tie the other end to a paper clip. Suspend the string and paper clip into the solution, with the pencil serving as an anchor on the rim of the jar, as shown in Figure 2.

   The string should only go down two thirds of the length of the jar so that the clip is hanging in the solution and not touching the bottom of the jar.

8. Leave the jar undisturbed for seven days at room temperature.

Figure 2.

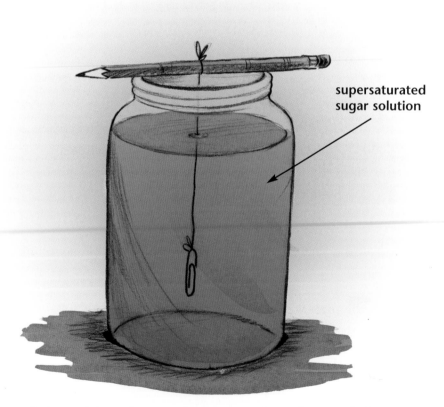

supersaturated
sugar solution

Sugar crystals can be grown from a supersaturated sugar solution.

Results and Conclusions

After seven days you should see clearly defined sugar crystals on the string. You can continue to let them grow or eat them! You've made rock candy.

The supersaturated solution you made contained more sugar than could normally dissolve in the water. As the water evaporated, the solution became even more saturated and sugar molecules began to come out of solution, forming crystals molecule by molecule.

 Science Project Ideas

- Look at a few granules of sugar under a microscope. Compare their shape with the shape of the sugar crystals you grew. What do you find?

- Try the same procedure used in this experiment to grow crystals made from other chemicals such as salt, baking soda, and alum. (All can be found in a grocery store.) Compare the shapes of these crystals with those of sugar, but do not eat these crystals!

CHAPTER 2

Compounds of Carbon

Scientists once thought that organic (carbon) compounds could be made only by living plants or animals. However, in 1828, Friederich Wöhler (1800–1882), a German chemist, put together urea. Urea is an organic compound normally found in urine. He prepared it by reacting two inorganic compounds, ammonium chloride and silver cyanate.

Today, thousands of carbon compounds not found in living organisms are prepared in laboratories throughout the world. These compounds include medicines, textiles, dyes, perfumes, paints, vitamins, detergents, and hormones.

In the early 1800s English chemist John Dalton (1766–1844) developed an explanation of matter. He proposed that elements such as hydrogen, oxygen or carbon are made up of tiny indivisible, indestructible particles called atoms.

◄ Diamond is a form of carbon. It is the hardest naturally occurring substance.

Molecules, Atoms, and Chemical Bonds

Today we know that an atom does have parts. It has a center, called a nucleus (plural: nuclei), which is made up of protons. Protons have a positive electric charge. There are also neutrons in the atom's nucleus (except for most hydrogen atoms, which do not have neutrons). Neutrons carry no charge and are approximately equal in weight to protons. Traveling around the nucleus, like planets around the sun, are electrons, which have a negative electric charge. Electrons weigh only about 1/2,000 the weight of a proton or neutron.

All the atoms of any given element have the same number of protons and electrons. The numbers of protons and electrons in the atoms of each element are different from the number in every other element. For example, only hydrogen atoms have one proton and one electron; only oxygen atoms have eight protons and eight electrons; only carbon atoms have six protons and six electrons.

The number of neutrons in the nuclei may differ, however. In the case of hydrogen, most of its atoms' nuclei contain one proton and no neutrons. A small fraction of hydrogen atoms have nuclei with one neutron as well as a proton. An even smaller percentage of hydrogen atoms have two neutrons as well as a proton in their nuclei.

The atoms of an element that differ in the number of neutrons they contain are called isotopes. The isotopes of hydrogen, helium, and oxygen are shown in Figure 3. The symbols for atoms of hydrogen, helium, and oxygen are H, He, and O.

Figure 3.

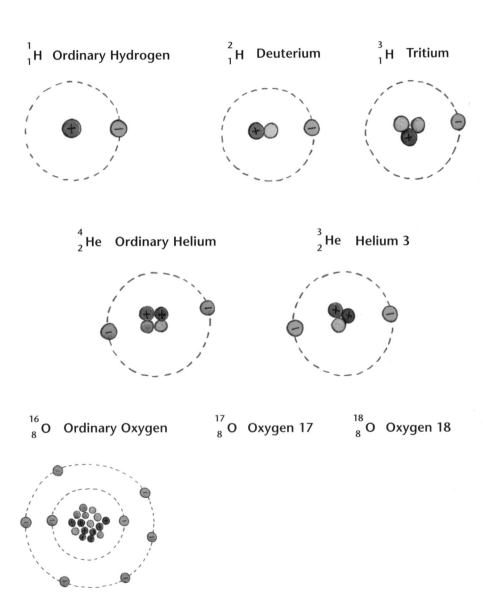

These drawings illustrate the isotopes of hydrogen and helium, and one of oxygen's isotopes. On a separate sheet of paper, see if you can draw the other two isotopes of oxygen.

The lower number in front of the symbol tells the number of protons in the atom's nucleus. This number is known as the element's atomic number. The upper number in front of the symbol tells us the number of protons plus neutrons in the nucleus. This is the atom's atomic weight.

An atom's electrons are in shells that surround the nucleus. The first shell can hold only two electrons, while the second shell can hold up to eight electrons. Oxygen atoms have eight electrons: two in the first shell and six in the second shell. A third shell can hold up to 18 electrons, a fourth shell up to 32 electrons, and a fifth shell even more.

Uranium, the heaviest natural atom, has 92 electrons and 92 protons. Uranium isotopes have atomic weights of 234, 235, 236, and 238. How many neutrons are in the nuclei of each of uranium's isotopes? Uranium isotope 235 has a nucleus that can split. When it does, it releases lots of energy. The fission (splitting) of many such nuclei is the basis for the atomic bomb and also produces power for nuclear energy.

Carbon, the element found in all organic compounds, has six protons and six electrons. The nucleus of carbon's most common isotope contains six neutrons. The nuclei of its other two isotopes have seven or eight neutrons. Using Figure 3 as a guide, see if you can illustrate the three isotopes of carbon. (For answer, see page 156.)

Some atoms can donate electrons to other atoms. Such atoms become bonded to one another to form compounds. Such a bond is known as an ionic bond. Figure 4a shows how an ionic bond is formed. An atom of lithium transfers its outermost electron to an atom of fluorine. This results in the formation of two ions (charged atoms). The lithium acquires a positive charge and the fluorine a negative charge. (Remember that like charges—both positive or both negative—repel each other. Unlike charges—a positive and a negative—are attracted to each other.) The resulting ions attract one another and form a stable salt, lithium fluoride (LiF). Many compounds, such as ordinary salt (sodium chloride, NaCl), exist as ions.

Acids and Bases

Certain ions make a substance either acidic or basic. Acids are substances that donate their protons (H^+), and bases are substances that can accept protons. Acids form hydrogen ions (H^+) and bases form hydroxide ions (OH^-). When acids and bases react, they form a salt and water in a process called neutralization.

However, when carbon combines with other elements, its atoms *share* electrons with the atoms of the other element or elements. Such bonds are called *covalent bonds*. Figure 4b shows a carbon atom sharing its four outer electrons with one

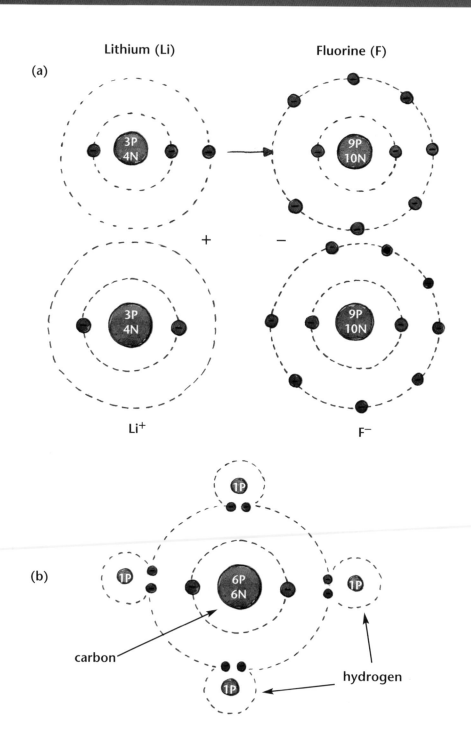

electron from each of four hydrogen atoms. The result is a molecule of methane (CH_4) that has four covalent bonds. The chemical formula, CH_4, shows that a molecule of methane is made up of one carbon atom and four hydrogen atoms. By sharing electrons, the carbon in methane now has the maximum number of electrons it can hold in its second shell (8), and each hydrogen atom has the maximum number its first shell can hold (2).

Figure 4.

a) A lithium atom transfers an electron to a fluorine atom to form an ionic bond. In so doing, a positive lithium ion (Li^+) and a negative fluoride ion (F^-) are formed.

b) A carbon atom shares the four electrons in its outer shell with the four electrons of four hydrogen atoms to form four covalent bonds in a molecule of methane (CH_4).

EXPERIMENT 2.1

Molecular Models

Question:

How are the bonded atoms of carbon and hydrogen arranged in space?

Hypothesis:

A three-dimensional model will show that their bonds tend to be as far apart as possible.

Materials:

- ball-and-stick chemical models, or different colored gumdrops and toothpicks

The diagram in Figure 4b shows four covalent bonds in methane. But it doesn't show how the bonded atoms of carbon and hydrogen are arranged in space. Atoms do combine to form many stable molecules by sharing electrons. However, because all electrons carry a negative charge, the two electrons in each bond repel the electrons in other bonds. (Remember, like charges repel.) Consequently, the bonds that form tend to be as far apart as possible.

You may be able to borrow ball-and-stick chemical models from your school's science department. Otherwise, make your own three-dimensional model to show what the methane molecule might look like.

You can use gumdrops and toothpicks.

Procedure:

1. A black gumdrop can represent a carbon atom. Four gumdrops of another color can represent hydrogen atoms.

2. Toothpicks can represent the bonds between the carbon and the four hydrogen atoms that form the molecule of methane.

Figure 5.

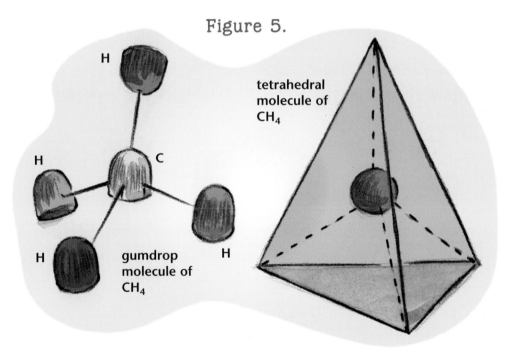

H

tetrahedral molecule of CH_4

H   C

H

H   gumdrop molecule of CH_4 H

This gumdrop model of a methane molecule shows its shape is a tetrahedron. This tetrahedral shape allows the covalent bonds to have maximum separation.

Results and Conclusions

If you place the bonds as far apart as possible, you'll find that you've made a molecule like the one in Figure 5. The overall shape of that molecule is a tetrahedron.

If you let yet a different colored gumdrop represent fluorine or chlorine atoms, you can form molecules of carbon tetrafluoride (CF_4) or carbon tetrachloride (CCl_4).

 Science Project Idea

- Devise other ways to make molecular models.

EXPERIMENT 2.2

Ionic and Covalent Bonds

Question:

Do ionic compounds (salt water) conduct electricity? Do covalent compounds (sugar water) conduct electricity?

Hypothesis:

Compounds formed by ionic bonds will conduct electricity. Compounds formed by covalent bonds will not conduct electricity.

Materials:

- clear plastic vial
- table salt
- paper clips
- 6-volt dry-cell battery or 4 D cells and a mailing tube and masking tape
- 3 wires, preferably with alligator clips
- flashlight bulb
- socket (holder) for flashlight bulb (optional)
- clothespins
- water
- wooden coffee stirrer
- sugar
- cooking oil

Procedure:

1. Nearly fill a clear plastic vial with table salt. Table salt is sodium chloride, which has equal numbers of sodium ions (Na^+) and chloride ions (Cl^-).

2. Slide two paper clips onto the top of the vial as shown in Figure 6a. Half of each paper clip should be inside the vial. The paper clips will serve as electrodes.

3. Use wires with alligator clips to connect the paper-clip electrodes to a 6-volt dry-cell battery and a flashlight bulb in a socket, as shown.

   If you don't have such a battery, you can make one by placing four D cells head to tail (Figure 6b) in a mailing tube. The tube should be slightly shorter than the total length of the four D cells. Use masking tape to fasten paper clips firmly against the positive and negative terminals at each end of the battery, as shown.

4. If you don't have a socket (holder) for the bulb, touch the metal base of the bulb with one wire and the metal side with a second wire, as shown in Figure 6c. If necessary, use clothespins to hold the ends of the wires in place.

   Does the bulb light? Does solid table salt conduct electricity?

   The ions in a solid aren't free to move; they're in fixed positions. But suppose you dissolve some of the salt in water so that the ions can move. Will the solution conduct electricity?

5. To find out, remove half the solid salt from the vial, add water to nearly fill it, and stir with a wooden coffee stirrer to dissolve as much of the salt as possible.

6. Again, connect the paper clips to the battery and a light bulb. Does the bulb light now? What does this tell you?

Table sugar (sucrose) is an organic compound. Its molecules contain 45 atoms of carbon, hydrogen, and oxygen joined to one another by covalent bonds. The chemical formula for sucrose is $C_{12}H_{22}O_{11}$. Can you account for the 45 atoms? Do you think a sugar solution will conduct electricity when dissolved in water?

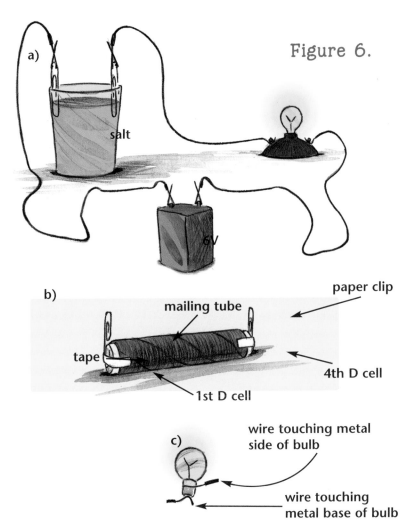

Figure 6.

a)

salt

b)

mailing tube

paper clip

tape

4th D cell

1st D cell

c)

wire touching metal side of bulb

wire touching metal base of bulb

a) This circuit can be used to test substances to see if they conduct electricity.

b) Four D cells end to end can be used to make a 6-volt battery.

c) If bulb sockets are not available, touch the metal base of the bulb with one wire and the metal side of the bulb with a second wire.

7. To find out, half fill the vial you used before with sugar. Add water until the vial is nearly full. Stir to make a solution of sugar.

8. Connect the paper-clip electrodes to the battery and light bulb. Does the sugar solution conduct electricity? Was your prediction correct?

9. Clean and dry the vial. Then nearly fill it with cooking oil. Add the paper clips and repeat the experiment. Does cooking oil conduct electricity? Do you think cooking oil contains ionic or covalent bonds?

Results and Conclusions

Since compounds formed by ionic bonds consist of charged atoms (ions), they conduct electricity. On the other hand, the molecules of compounds with covalent bonds aren't charged, so they do not conduct electricity, or they conduct it very poorly. Electricity is the flow of electrons from one atom to another. The atoms in the molecules of the most common covalent bonds share electron pairs, making it impossible or difficult for electrons to flow freely.

EXPERIMENT 2.3

Models of Other Organic Molecules

Question:

Can carbon atoms bond with other carbon atoms?

Hypothesis:

Yes, and they can form long chains.

Materials:

- ball-and-stick chemical models or gumdrops and toothpicks
- pen or pencil and paper

Ethane is a simple organic compound. Its molecules consist of two carbon atoms and six hydrogen atoms (C_2H_6). Diagrams of ethane and methane molecules are shown in Figure 7a. The small circles represent electrons.

Figure 7b shows another way to represent covalent bonds using a simple line to represent two electrons. In these representations only the electrons in the outer shells are shown, because they are the only ones involved in bonding. You can think of ethane as two methane molecules that unite after each loses an atom of hydrogen.

Procedure:

1. See if you can make a model of ethane using ball-and-stick models or gumdrops and toothpicks. Remember the tetrahedral nature of covalent bonding with carbon.

   Compounds with three- and four-carbon chains, propane and butane, are shown in Figure 7c. In Figure 7d, compounds with from five- to ten-carbon chains are shown without their attached hydrogens.

2. Try to complete the drawings of these molecules on a separate sheet of paper. (For the answer, see page 156.)

   In the molecules of some compounds, carbon atoms share more than one electron with another carbon atom. For example, in ethene, or ethylene (C_2H_4; see Figure 8a), each carbon atom shares two electrons with the other. Such a covalent bond is referred to as a double bond. It can be represented by two short lines. In ethyne, more commonly known as acetylene (C_2H_2), each carbon shares three electrons to form a triple bond, as shown in Figure 8b.

3. Use ball-and-stick chemical models or gumdrops and toothpicks to form molecular models of ethene and ethyne.

   Double and triple bonds are not limited to carbon-carbon bonding. For example, acetic acid ($C_2H_4O_2$), the acid we commonly call vinegar, has a double bond between a carbon and an oxygen atom, as shown in Figure 8c.

4. Prepare a model of a molecule of acetic acid.

5. Draw what you think are the bonds between carbon and oxygen in carbon dioxide (CO_2) and carbon monoxide (CO).

6. Then make models of the molecules of these two compounds.

a)

```
      H                    H   H
      ..                   ..  ..
   H : C : H            H : C : C : H
      ..                   ..  ..
      H                    H   H
   methane                 ethane
```

b)

```
      H                    H   H
      |                    |   |
   H – C – H            H – C – C – H
      |                    |   |
      H                    H   H
   methane                 ethane
```

c)

```
   H   H   H            H   H   H   H
   |   |   |            |   |   |   |
H – C – C – C – H    H – C – C – C – C – H
   |   |   |            |   |   |   |
   H   H   H            H   H   H   H
     propane                 butane
```

d)

```
   C – C – C – C – C        C – C – C – C – C – C
        pentane                    hexane

C – C – C – C – C – C – C     C – C – C – C – C – C – C – C
        heptane                        octane

        C – C – C – C – C – C – C – C – C
                      nonane

       C – C – C – C – C – C – C – C – C – C
                      decane
```

Figure 7.

a) The shared electrons in the covalent bonds in methane and ethane molecules are represented by black dots.

b) The covalent bonds in methane and ethane can also be represented by short lines (dashes). Each dash represents two electrons.

c) Propane and butane are the next two compounds in the alkane series of hydrocarbons.

d) The next six compounds in the alkane series are shown as chains of carbon atoms joined by covalent bonds. On a separate sheet of paper, can you add the hydrogen atoms?

Results and Conclusions

One of the properties of carbon is its ability to bond with other carbon atoms, forming long chains. Carbon is so effective at forming covalent bonds with other atoms that carbon compounds make up the majority of all chemical compounds. It's estimated there are at least ten million known carbon compounds.

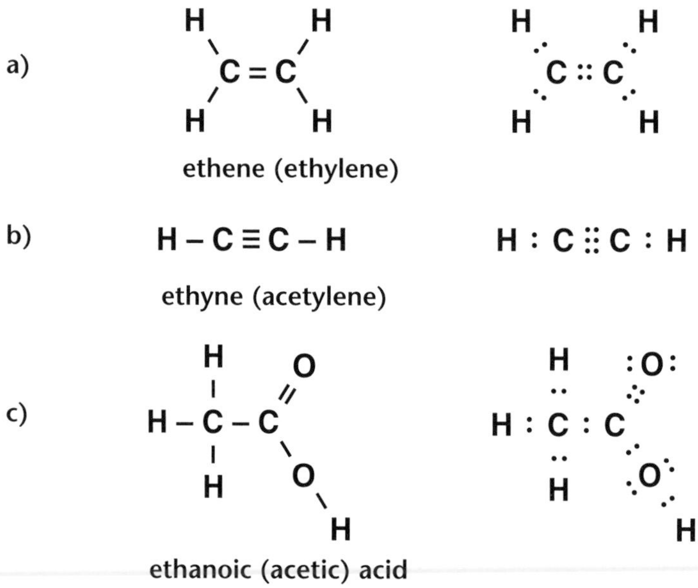

a)

$$H \quad H \qquad\qquad H \quad H$$
$$\underset{H}{\overset{H}{\diagdown}} C = C \overset{H}{\underset{H}{\diagup}} \qquad\qquad C :: C$$

ethene (ethylene)

b) $H - C \equiv C - H \qquad\qquad H : C :: C : H$

ethyne (acetylene)

c)

$$\begin{array}{cc} H & O \\ | & \| \\ H - C - C & \\ | & \diagdown \\ H & O \\ & \diagdown \\ & H \end{array}$$

ethanoic (acetic) acid

Figure 8.

a) Carbon atoms form a double bond by sharing four electrons in ethene, or ethylene, the first hydrocarbon in the alkene series.
b) Carbon atoms form a triple bond by sharing six electrons in ethyne, or acetylene, the first hydrocarbon in the alkyne series.
c) Acetic acid molecules contain a double bond between a carbon atom and an oxygen atom.

EXPERIMENT 2.4

Alkenes and Alkynes

Question:

How do hydrocarbons get their names?

Hypothesis:

The scientific system of naming hydrocarbons uses the number of carbon atoms in the molecule and the type of bond forming the chain of carbon atoms.

Materials:

- ball-and-stick chemical models or gumdrops and toothpicks
- pen or pencil and paper

Hydrocarbons

Compounds consisting of only the elements carbon and hydrogen are called hydrocarbons. Hydrocarbons make up the oil pumped from the earth. They are the compounds in gasoline, kerosene, diesel, and various other fuels, including natural gas. They are also the starting points for making dyes, explosives, plastics, and aspirin as well as many other drugs.

The compounds in what is known as the alkane series of hydrocarbons have only single bonds. Part of this series, from methane to decane, was shown in Figure 7. All compounds in the alkane series have the general formula $C_nH_{2n + 2}$. The n represents the number of carbon atoms in the molecule; the number of hydrogen atoms is equal to twice the number of carbon atoms plus 2, that is, $2n + 2$. For example, ethane (C_2H_6) has 2 carbon atoms, so $n = 2$. Therefore, the number of hydrogen atoms will be $2 \times 2 + 2 = 6$. How many hydrogen atoms will there be in decane, which has 10 carbon atoms? (For the answer, see page 156.)

The alkene series of hydrocarbons are those that have one double bond in the chain of carbon atoms. The general formula for the alkenes is C_nH_{2n}. For example, propene is a three-carbon chain molecule; therefore, $n = 3$, and so the number of hydrogen atoms in propene is 6 (2×3). A number of compounds in the alkene series are shown in Figure 9a.

Hydrocarbons in the alkyne series have one triple bond in the chain of carbon atoms. The general formula for the alkynes is C_nH_{2n-2}. For example, butyne is a four-carbon chain molecule; therefore, $n = 4$. The number of hydrogen atoms in butyne is 6 ($2 \times 4 - 2$). A number of compounds in the alkyne series are shown in Figure 9b.

a)

```
     H  H            H  H  H              H  H  H  H
     |  |            |  |  |              |  |  |  |
  H – C = C       H – C = C – C – H    H – C = C – C – C – H
        |               |                       |  |
        H               H                       H  H
    ethene            propene                  butene
```

```
     |  |  |  |  |              |  |  |  |  |  |
   – C = C – C – C – C –      – C = C – C – C – C – C –
              |  |  |                    |  |  |  |
         pentene                      hexene
```

```
          |  |  |  |  |  |  |
        – C = C – C – C – C – C – C –
                   |  |  |  |  |
                 heptene
```

```
   |  |  |  |  |  |  |  |          |  |  |  |  |  |  |  |  |
 – C = C – C – C – C – C – C – C –   – C = C – C – C – C – C – C – C – C –
   |  |  |  |  |  |                  |  |  |  |  |  |  |
      octene                              nonene
```

```
          |  |  |  |  |  |  |  |  |  |
        – C = C – C – C – C – C – C – C – C – C –
          |  |  |  |  |  |  |  |  |
                  decene
```

b)

```
                                              H
                                              |
      H – C ≡ C – H         H – C ≡ C – C – H
         ethyne                propyne     |
                                           H
```

```
        H  H                      H  H  H
        |  |                      |  |  |
   H – C ≡ C – C – C – H     H – C ≡ C – C – C – C – H
            |  |                      |  |  |
            H  H                      H  H  H
       butyne                       pentyne
```

```
        |  |  |  |  |              |  |  |  |  |
      – C ≡ C – C – C – C – C –   – C ≡ C – C – C – C – C – C –
              |  |  |  |                   |  |  |  |  |
         hexyne                          heptyne
```

```
   |  |  |  |  |  |  |              |  |  |  |  |  |  |  |
 – C ≡ C – C – C – C – C – C – C –   – C ≡ C – C – C – C – C – C – C – C –
   |  |  |  |  |  |                  |  |  |  |  |  |  |
      octyne                              nonyne
```

```
          |  |  |  |  |  |  |  |
        – C ≡ C – C – C – C – C – C – C – C – C –
          |  |  |  |  |  |  |  |
                  decyne
```

Figure 9.

a) These diagrams show the alkene series from ethene to decene.
b) The alkyne series from ethyne to decyne is shown in these diagrams.

Procedure:

1. Use Figures 9a and 9b to prepare molecular models of ethene, propene, ethyne, and propyne.

2. Then, on a separate sheet of paper, complete the drawings of the alkene series from pentene to decene and the alkyne series from hexyne to decyne.

3. Finally, show that the formulas C_nH_{2n+2}, C_nH_{2n}, and C_nH_{2n-2} work for all the compounds shown in Figures 7 and 9.

Results and Conclusions

Why do you think there are no compounds named methene and methyne? This is because the *meth-* prefix indicates one carbon atom. For there to be double or triple bonds there must be at least two carbon atoms in the molecule.

The prefixes *meth-*, *eth-*, *pro-*, *but-*, *pent-*, *hex-*, *hept-*, *oct-*, *non-*, and *dec-* for the alkane, alkene, and alkyne series of hydrocarbons originate in the Greek words for the numbers 1 through 10. These prefixes tell us the number of carbon atoms in the molecule.

EXPERIMENT 2.5

Isomers

Question:

Do all compounds with the same chemical formula have the same arrangement of atoms?

Hypothesis:

No. Some compounds with the same chemical formula differ in the way their atoms are arranged.

Materials:

- ball-and-stick chemical models or gumdrops and toothpicks

Isomers are compounds that have the same chemical formula but their atoms are arranged differently. For example, the compound C_4H_{10} shown in Figure 10a can exist as normal butane (n-butane) or as isobutane. Their characteristics also differ in that isobutane boils at $-11.6°C$, melts at $-159.4°C$, and has a density of 0.55 g/mL, while n-butane boils at $-0.5°C$, melts at $-138.4°C$, and has a density of 0.60 g/mL.

Procedure:

1. Using ball-and-stick chemical models or gumdrops and toothpicks, make molecular models of the two isomers *n*-butane and isobutane.

2. Next, make molecular models of C_5H_{12} to show that in addition to *n*-pentane there are two other isomers of this compound.

3. Use ball-and-stick chemical models or gumdrops and toothpicks to show that there are no isomers of methyl chloride because all the structural formulas in Figure 10b are identical.

4. Go on to demonstrate, using molecular models, that there are two isomers of dichloroethane, $C_2H_4Cl_2$. One of those isomers is shown in Figure 10c.

Results and Conclusions

Although both forms of butane have four carbon and ten hydrogen atoms, their properties and structure are not identical.

As the length of the carbon chain in organic molecules increases, so does the number of possible isomers. Use models to show this structure.

a)

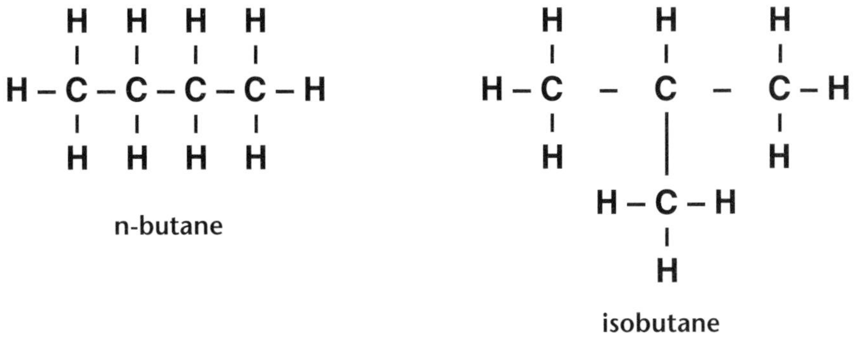

H   H   H   H
| | | |
H – C – C – C – C – H
| | | |
H   H   H   H

n-butane

H   H   H
| | |
H – C – C – C – H
| | |
H | H
    H – C – H
        |
        H

isobutane

b)

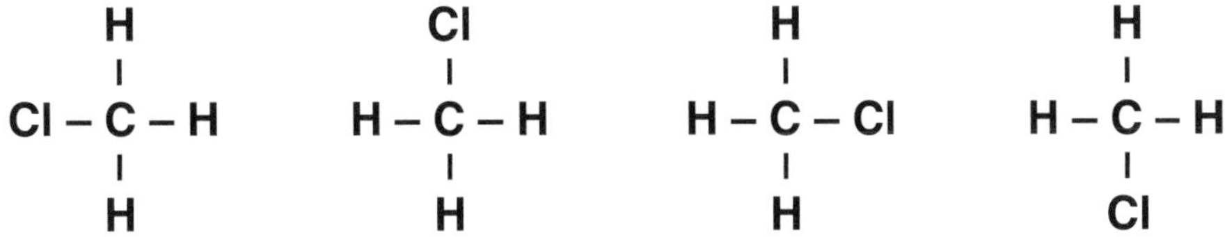

H   CI   H   H
| | | |
CI – C – H   H – C – H   H – C – CI   H – C – H
| | | |
H   H   H   CI

c)

H   H
| |
H – C – C – H
| |
CI CI

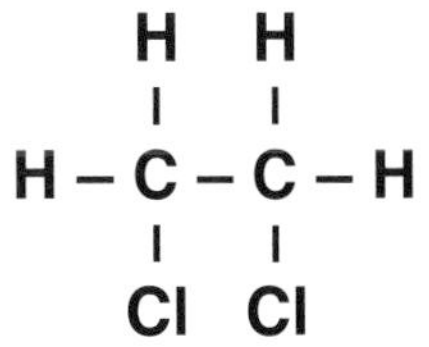

Figure 10.

a) These diagrams show the structural formulas of n-butane and isobutane.
b) These structural formulas of methyl chloride are all identical.
c) There are two isomers of dichloroethane. Only one of them is shown here. Can you draw the second one on a separate sheet of paper?

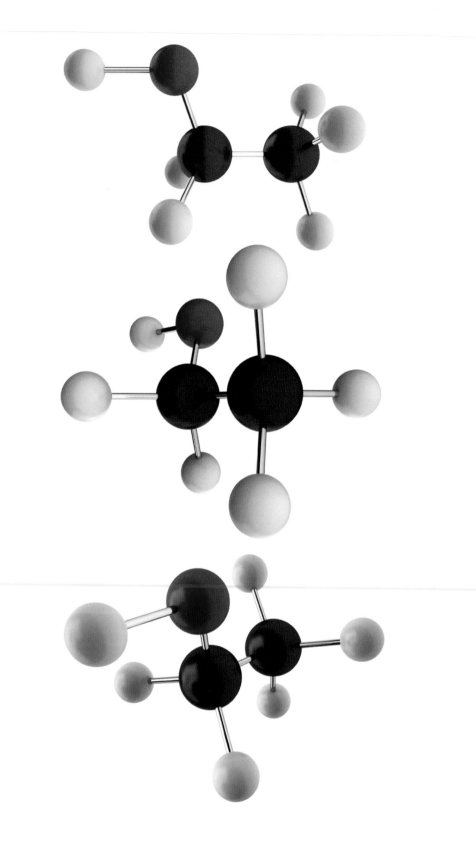

CHAPTER 3

Polar and Nonpolar Compounds

As you saw in Chapter 2, compounds in which atoms share electrons are described as having covalent bonds. In some compounds the electrons in the covalent molecules are not shared equally. They tend to be more concentrated at one end (pole) of the molecule than the other. This is true of water molecules. As shown in the diagram of a water molecule in Figure 11a, the angle between the two bonds that join the hydrogen atoms to the oxygen atom is 105 degrees.

◀ This is a model of three ethanol molecules. Ethanol's chemical formula is C_2H_5OH.

However, the oxygen atom has a stronger attraction for the shared electrons than do the hydrogen atoms. As a result, the oxygen end of the molecule is slightly negative, while the hydrogen end has a slight positive charge. We say that the molecule is polar.

Because water molecules are polar, the hydrogen (+) end of the molecule is attracted to the oxygen (−) end of other water molecules. As illustrated in Figure 11b, these attractive forces create weak bonds, called hydrogen bonds, between water molecules.

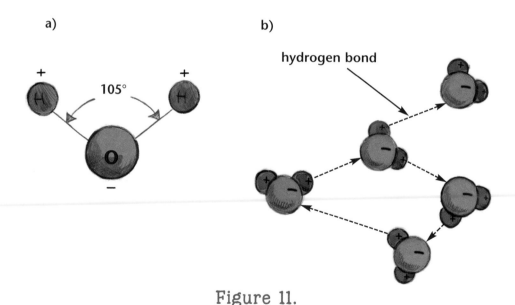

Figure 11.

a) In water molecules, hydrogen atoms bond to oxygen at an angle of 105 degrees.

b) The polar molecules of water are attracted to one another through weak hydrogen bonds.

EXPERIMENT 3.1

Polar and Nonpolar Compounds

Question:

Is it easy to show whether liquid molecules are polar or nonpolar?

Hypothesis:

The polar nature of various molecules of liquid can be demonstrated with just an electrically charged plastic comb.

Materials:

- plastic comb
- paper towel or wool cloth
- water faucet
- cooking oil
- sink
- finishing nail
- Styrofoam cups
- a partner
- rubbing alcohol
- propanol or ethanol (optional)
- dinner fork
- paper clip
- bowl
- plastic vial or small glass
- eyedroppers
- waxed paper
- toothpicks

Procedure:

1. Charge a plastic comb by rubbing it with a paper towel or wool cloth.

2. Bring the comb near a thin stream of water flowing from a faucet. What happens to the stream? Would it make any difference whether the comb was positively or negatively charged?

3. Now, over a sink, repeat the experiment with a thin stream of cooking oil. To obtain a thin stream of cooking oil, use a finishing nail to make a small hole in the bottom of a Styrofoam cup.

4. Have a partner hold the cup with his or her finger over the small opening while you pour some cooking oil into the cup.

5. Charge the comb as before and have your friend move the finger so that a thin stream of oil flows into another cup several feet below the opening.

   Does the stream bend when you hold the charged comb near it, as shown in Figure 12? What can you conclude about the molecules of cooking oil?

6. Repeat the experiment using rubbing alcohol and a new Styrofoam cup. What happens this time? Can you conclude that the molecules of rubbing alcohol are polar?

Results and Conclusions

Rubbing alcohol is 70 percent isopropanol (also called isopropyl alcohol) and 30 percent water. So the effect you saw could have been due to the water in the mixture. If possible, obtain some pure propanol or ethanol (ethyl alcohol) and repeat the experiment. What do you find?

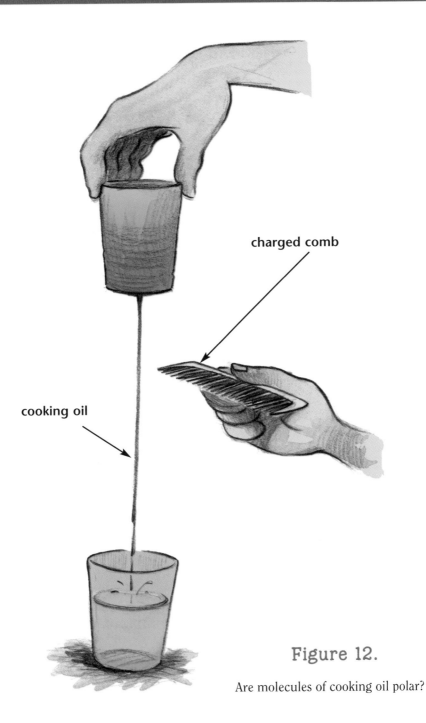

charged comb

cooking oil

Figure 12.

Are molecules of cooking oil polar?

In the water experiment, it would make no difference whether the comb was positively or negatively charged. Both ends of the water molecule have a charge; either one or the other will be attracted to the charged comb. The response of various liquids to the electrical charge of the comb demonstrates whether their molecules have more or less polarity than water.

Polarity of Water

The polarity of water molecules causes them to attract one another. The attractive forces between their molecules causes water to pull together. The tendency of water to hold together creates a "skin" on the surface, a property called surface tension.

Procedure:

1. To see how well water holds together, use a clean dinner fork to gently place a paper clip on the surface of some clean water in a bowl. Notice that the paper clip doesn't sink. But if you look closely, you will see that it does bend the water's "skin."

2. To see another effect of the polarity of water molecules, fill a plastic vial or small glass with water.

3. Then, using an eyedropper, see how high you can heap the water above the edge of the vessel.

4. To demonstrate still another effect of water's polarity, use a clean eyedropper to place a drop of water on a sheet of waxed paper. Notice the round shape of the drop when viewed from the side. Place a second drop of water close to the first one. Then use a toothpick to slowly move the second drop closer to the first one.

Results and Conclusions

What happens immediately when the two drops touch? Repeat these three experiments using cooking oil in place of water. How might you expect the results to differ? How do they differ?

 Science Project Idea

• Design and carry out an experiment to measure the surface tension of different liquids.

EXPERIMENT 3.2

Polarity, Alcohols, and Organic Acids

Question:

Are common alcohols such as methanol, ethanol, propanol, and isopropanol polar?

Hypothesis:

You can find out whether these alcohols are polar by making chemical models.

Materials:

- **an adult**
- ball-and-stick chemical models or gumdrops and toothpicks
- baking soda (NaHCO$_3$)
- vinegar (CH$_3$COOH)
- 10 mL graduated cylinder
- teaspoon
- drinking glass
- matches
- pen or pencil and paper

Procedure:

Use ball-and-stick chemical models or gumdrops and toothpicks to prepare a model of methanol (methyl alcohol). The structural formulas for methanol, ethanol, propanol, isopropanol, and water are shown in Figure 13a.

Figure 13.

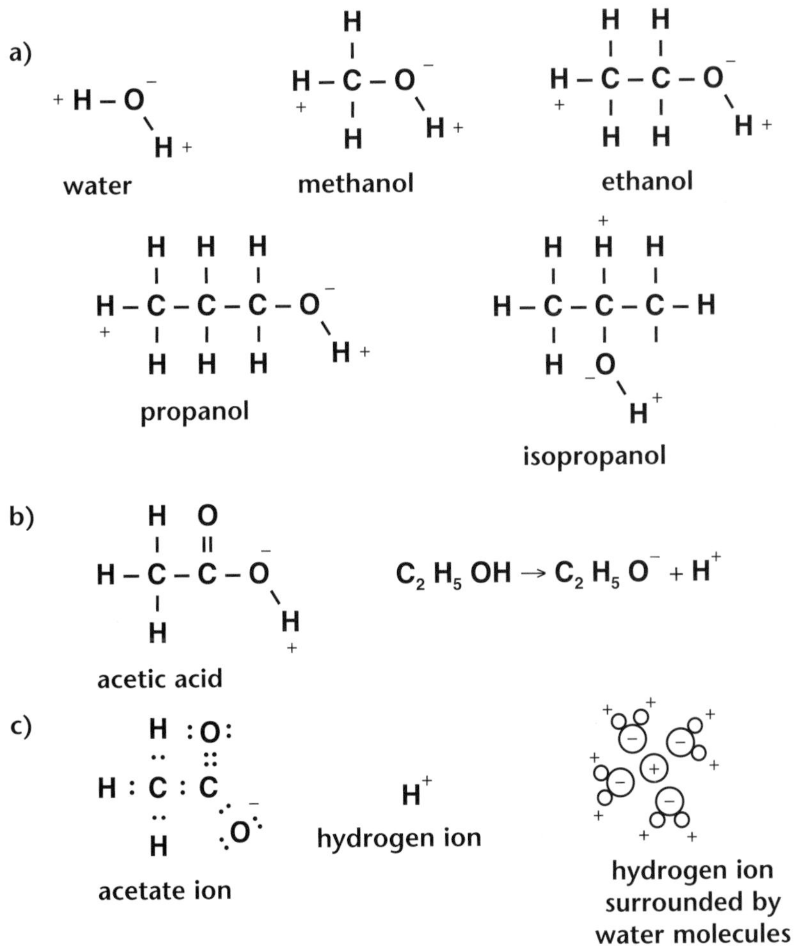

a)

+ H – O⁻
        \
         H +

water

$$H-\underset{\underset{H}{|}}{\overset{\overset{H}{|}}{C}}-O^-$$
+   \
                H +

methanol

$$H-\underset{\underset{H}{|}}{\overset{\overset{H}{|}}{C}}-\underset{\underset{H}{|}}{\overset{\overset{H}{|}}{C}}-O^-$$
+   \
                           H +

ethanol

$$H-\underset{\underset{H}{|}}{\overset{\overset{H}{|}}{C}}-\underset{\underset{H}{|}}{\overset{\overset{H}{|}}{C}}-\underset{\underset{H}{|}}{\overset{\overset{H}{|}}{C}}-O^-$$
+   \
                                      H +

propanol

$$H-\underset{\underset{H}{|}}{\overset{\overset{H}{|}}{C}}-\underset{\underset{O}{|}}{\overset{\overset{H}{|}}{C}}-\underset{\underset{H}{|}}{\overset{\overset{H}{|}}{C}}-H$$
                          \
                           H⁺

isopropanol

b)

$$H-\underset{\underset{H}{|}}{\overset{\overset{H}{|}}{C}}-\underset{}{\overset{\overset{O}{\|}}{C}}-O^-$$
                        \
                         H
                          +

acetic acid

$$C_2 H_5\, OH \rightarrow C_2 H_5\, O^- + H^+$$

c)

H :O:
¨ ¨
H : C : C
¨   ¨
H   :O:⁻

acetate ion

H⁺

hydrogen ion

hydrogen ion surrounded by water molecules

a) Like water, alcohols have polar molecules.
b) The same is true of organic acids such as ethanoic acid, commonly called acetic acid.
c) Acetic acid forms hydrogen ions in water.

Results and Conclusions

From your model, you can see that the methanol molecule can be thought of as a water molecule in which one hydrogen atom has been replaced by a CH_3- group. A two-carbon or three-carbon chain with associated hydrogen atoms appears in the case of ethanol, propanol, or isopropanol.

Many organic acids (those containing carbon) form hydrogen ions (H^+) in water. Organic acids have a $-COOH$ group at one end of the molecule. The acetic acid molecule (Figure 13b) shows this pattern. The acid's hydrogen atom attracts the oxygen ends of water molecules. In some of the acetic acid molecules, this hydrogen atom is pulled away from the rest of the molecule. When this happens, the hydrogen atom leaves its electron with the molecule. The result is a hydrogen ion (H^+) and a negative organic ion (an ion containing carbon). In the case of acetic acid, the negative ion is the acetate ion shown in Figure 13c. The hydrogen ion (H^+) gives the acid its characteristic properties. These properties include a sour taste, the ability to turn blue litmus paper red, and reactions with some metals and other substances such as baking soda.

Procedure:

1. Use ball-and-stick chemical models or gumdrops and toothpicks to prepare a model of acetic acid.

2. Also prepare water molecule models and use them to show how acetic acid is converted to hydrogen ions and acetate ions.

3. You can easily see the reaction between acetic acid (CH_3COOH) and baking soda $(NaHCO_3)$. Simply add about 10 mL of vinegar, which is a solution of acetic acid, to one teaspoon of baking soda in a drinking glass.

Results and Conclusions

What happens? What gas do you think is produced?

From the chemical formulas, you might think the gas produced could be oxygen (O_2), hydrogen (H_2), carbon monoxide (CO), or carbon dioxide (CO_2). It's not carbon monoxide, which is a poisonous gas.

Remembering that oxygen makes things burn faster, hydrogen burns in air, and carbon dioxide is used to extinguish fires, repeat the experiment.

Procedure:

1. As the gas is being produced, **ask an adult** to lower a burning match into the glass. What happens? Which gas can you conclude is being produced?

2. Now that you know what gas is produced, see if you can complete the chemical equation shown below. Write the equation on a separate sheet of paper.

$$\underbrace{CH_3COO^- + H^+}_{\text{vinegar}} + \underbrace{Na^+ + HCO_3^-}_{\text{baking soda}} \longrightarrow Na^+ + CH_3COO^- + ? + ?$$

Results and Conclusions

After you complete the equation, there should be as many atoms of each element on the right side of the arrow as there are on the left. Are there?
(For the answer, see page 156.)

EXPERIMENT 3.3

Polarity, Solubility, and Density

Question:

How do substances with covalent bonds and those with ionic bonds compare in their solubility in water?

Hypothesis:

In general, substances with covalent bonds are insoluble in water, while ionic and polar substances are soluble.

Materials:

- teaspoon
- salt (NaCl)
- water
- small glass
- cooking oil
- balance for weighing
- 100-mL graduated cylinder
- rubbing alcohol
- methanol
- ethanol
- small, tall jar with a screw-on cap
- vinegar
- an egg
- table knife
- cereal bowl
- sugar
- citric acid
- detergent
- mucilage (plant gum)

If a solid dissolves (disappears) when mixed with a liquid, we say the solid is *soluble* in the liquid. If little or none of the solid dissolves, we say it's *insoluble*. If two liquids dissolve in one another, we say they are *miscible*. If they don't dissolve in one another, we say they are *immiscible*. The general properties, including solubility, of polar and nonpolar compounds, are listed in Table 1.

Recall that salt (sodium chloride, NaCl) is a solid that consists of sodium ions (Na^+) and chloride ions (Cl^-). Looking at Table 1, would you expect salt to be soluble in water?

Table 1.
Properties of Polar and Nonpolar Compounds

Type of Compound	General Properties
polar	Ends of molecules carry a small electric charge opposite in sign.
	Tend to form ions in water.
	Chemical bonding may be ionic.
	Tend to be soluble in other polar compounds.
	Tend to be insoluble in nonpolar compounds.
nonpolar	Molecules are uniformly neutral.
	Do not form ions in water.
	Chemical bonds are covalent.
	Tend to be soluble in other nonpolar compounds.
	Tend to be insoluble in polar compounds.

Procedure:

1. To check your prediction, add a teaspoonful of salt to a small glass.

2. Add about 150 mL of water and stir the mixture. Does salt dissolve in water?

   As you found in Experiments 2.2 and 3.1, cooking oil appears to have covalent, nonpolar chemical bonds. Would you expect cooking oil to be soluble in water?

3. To find out, add a teaspoon of cooking oil to about 100 mL of water in a small glass.

4. Stir the two liquids.

   Do cooking oil and water dissolve in one another; that is, are they miscible?

Results and Conclusions

Substances with covalent bonds, such as hydrocarbons, are insoluble in water, while ionic and polar substances, such as salt, are soluble.

Density

Another property of substances is density. The density of a substance is its weight per volume. That is,

$$\text{density} = \frac{\text{weight}}{\text{volume}} \text{, or } D = \frac{W}{V}$$

For liquids, density is usually measured in grams per milliliter (g/mL). Which do you predict is less dense, water or cooking oil? Why? (For the answer, see page 156.)

Procedure:

1. To confirm your prediction, weigh a 100-mL graduated cylinder.

2. Fill the cylinder to the 100-mL line with water and reweigh. How many grams does 100 mL of water weigh? What is the density of water in g/mL?

3. Repeat the experiment using cooking oil. What is the density of cooking oil? Was your prediction correct?

4. Next, add some cooking oil to 100 mL of rubbing alcohol.

Results and Conclusions

Which do you think is more dense, alcohol or cooking oil? What makes you think so? Confirm your prediction by finding the density of rubbing alcohol. Is it more or less dense than cooking oil?

If you stir the mixture of cooking oil and alcohol, do the liquids dissolve in one another? If they dissolve to form a solution, the solution will be clear (you can see through it). Is this mixture clear? Leave the mixture overnight. What happens?

Do you think rubbing alcohol and water are miscible (soluble in one another)? What about methanol and water? Ethanol and water? Do all these liquids consist of polar molecules? Try mixing each of these alcohols with water. Do they dissolve in one another?

Procedure:

1. Find a small, tall jar with a screw-on cap.

2. Add vinegar to the jar until it's about ⅛ full.

3. Then add about twice as much cooking oil. Do vinegar and cooking oil appear to be miscible?

4. Put the cap on the jar. Then shake the jar in order to break up the liquids and mix them together.

Results and Conclusions

Notice the tiny droplets of cooking oil spread throughout the liquid. Such a mixture is called an emulsion. Let the emulsion sit for a few minutes. What happens to the two liquids over time? Why is this mixture called a temporary emulsion? Where else have you seen an emulsion? One example is an oil spill in the ocean. They are difficult to clean up because the wind and waves mix oil and seawater, forming an emulsion.

Procedure:

1. Separate the yolk of an egg from the white. This can be done by first cracking the egg around its center with a table knife. Hold the egg upright over a cereal bowl and remove the upper half of the shell. Some egg white will fall into the bowl when you remove the upper half of the shell.

2. Now carefully pour the yolk, trying not to break it, from one half of the shell to the other several times over the bowl. As you do so, more egg white will fall into the bowl.

3. When most of the egg white has been removed, pour the yolk into the mixture of oil and vinegar, put the cap back on the jar, and shake it again.

4. Let this mixture sit for a few minutes.

Results and Conclusions

Is this a more permanent emulsion? Why do you think the egg yolk is called an emulsifying agent?

Safety: *Always wash your hands after handling raw eggs, and rinse the egg down the drain.*

There are many other emulsifying agents. In place of the egg yolk, you might repeat the experiment using a few drops of detergent, or mucilage (plant gum), which contains gum arabic.

There are exceptions to the general rules about solubility. For example, ammonia (NH_3) is a covalent compound that is very soluble in water. Sucrose, ordinary table sugar ($C_{12}H_{22}O_{11}$), is a covalent compound that is also very soluble in water. Is it soluble in rubbing alcohol or methanol? Design and carry out an experiment to find out.

Citric acid (see Figure 14) has three –COOH groups. It looks like three acetic acid molecules joined together. Do you think citric acid is soluble in water? Do you think it's soluble in rubbing alcohol? How about in methanol? Experiment to find out.

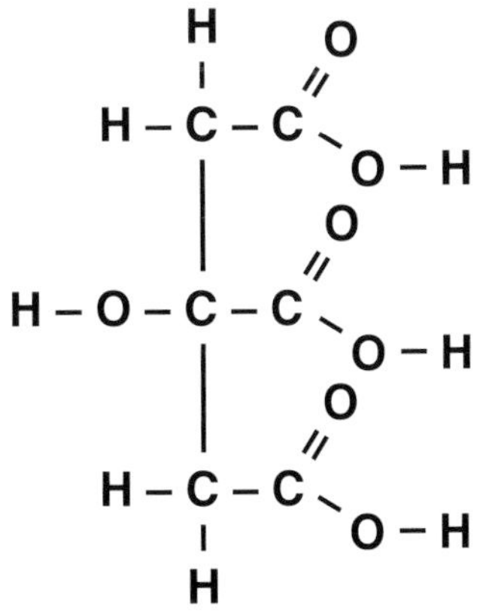

Figure 14.

This diagram shows the structural formula of citric acid.

citric acid ($C_6H_8O_7$)

Science Project Idea

- A suspension is a mixture that contains small particles of an insoluble solid dispersed through a liquid. You can make a very interesting suspension by putting 125 mL ($^1/_2$ cup) of cornstarch into a pan and adding half as much water. Mix the solid and liquid together with your hands. What happens when you try to squeeze a handful of the stuff? Try to pick up the mixture using a spoon. Put some of the suspension on a flat surface. What happens to it? Punch a small hole in a piece of paper and put some of the mixture over the hole. Does it leak through? What other properties do you notice about this strange stuff?

EXPERIMENT 3.4

Polarity, Soap, and Suds

Question:

Among water, soap, and detergent, which is the best substance to remove dirt from cotton fabric?

Hypothesis:

Soap combined with water will do the job, but detergent and water are most effective.

Materials:

- piece of cotton cloth
- dirt
- water
- hand soap
- detergent
- drinking straw
- test tube or vial

Fats, Soaps, Detergents, and Polar Molecules

The structural formula for a fat, glyceryl tristearate, is shown in Figure 15a. When a fat is boiled with sodium hydroxide (NaOH), also known as lye, an alcohol (glycerol) and a soap (sodium stearate) are produced. The chemical equation for that reaction is shown in Figure 15b.

In colonial America, and later on the frontier, people made soap by boiling wood ashes with animal fat. Wood ashes are rich in potassium carbonate (K_2CO_3), an alkaline (basic) substance that, like lye (NaOH), can react with fat to produce soap.

As Figure 16a reveals, one end of a soap molecule is a long hydrocarbon chain, which, like all hydrocarbons, is not soluble in water. The other end (−COONa) is polar and quite soluble in water. The hydrocarbon end of the soap molecule is hydrophobic, which means "water fearing." The polar end is hydrophilic, which means "water loving."

Procedure:

1. Find an old piece of cotton cloth and rub a section of it against some dirt on a floor or on the ground.

2. Pour some water onto the dirty spot and try to remove the dirt with water. Can water remove the dirty stain?

3. Now rub some moist hand soap into the stain and then rinse the soap away with water. What has happened to the dirty stain?

4. Repeat the experiment but this time use a detergent rather than soap.

Figure 15.

a)

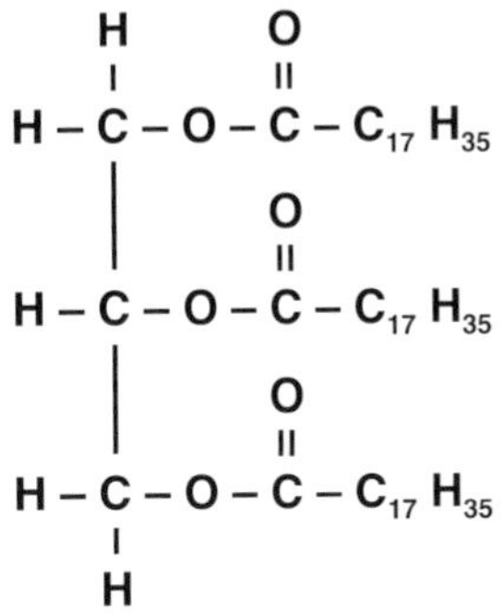

$$H-\overset{\overset{\displaystyle H}{|}}{C}-O-\overset{\overset{\displaystyle O}{||}}{C}-C_{17}\,H_{35}$$

$$H-C-O-\overset{\overset{\displaystyle O}{||}}{C}-C_{17}\,H_{35}$$

$$H-\underset{\underset{\displaystyle H}{|}}{C}-O-\overset{\overset{\displaystyle O}{||}}{C}-C_{17}\,H_{35}$$

b)

$$H-\overset{\overset{\displaystyle H}{|}}{C}-O-\overset{\overset{\displaystyle O}{||}}{C}-C_{17}H_{35}$$
$$H-C-O-\overset{\overset{\displaystyle O}{||}}{C}-C_{17}H_{35} \;+\; 3NaOH \;\rightarrow\; H-C-O-H \;+\; 3H_{35}C_{17}-\overset{\overset{\displaystyle O}{||}}{C}-O-Na$$
$$H-\underset{\underset{\displaystyle H}{|}}{C}-O-\overset{\overset{\displaystyle O}{||}}{C}-C_{17}H_{35} \qquad H-\underset{\underset{\displaystyle H}{|}}{C}-O-H$$

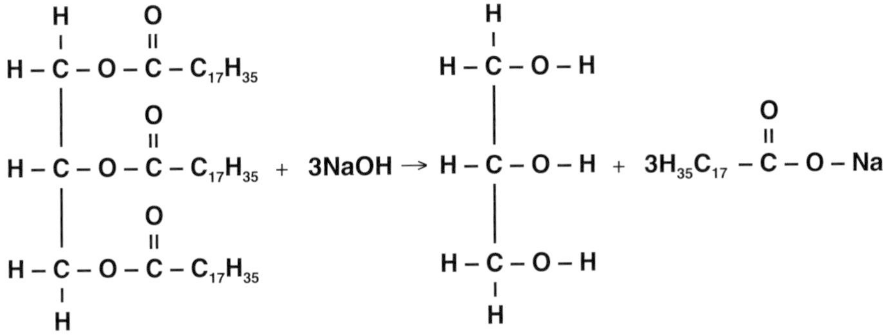

a) This diagram shows the structural formula of a fat, glyceryl tristearate.
b) This fat reacts with sodium hydroxide to form glycerol, an alcohol, and sodium stearate, a soap.

Results and Conclusions

Since most stains, such as grease and dirt, are made of nonpolar molecules, they cannot be dissolved and carried away by water. However, dirt and stains that are nonpolar are soluble in the hydrophobic end of soap molecules. But the soap molecule's hydrophilic end is soluble in water. As a result, the soap molecules bring the dirt and water together so that they can be washed away from clothes or other stained materials. (See Figure 16b.)

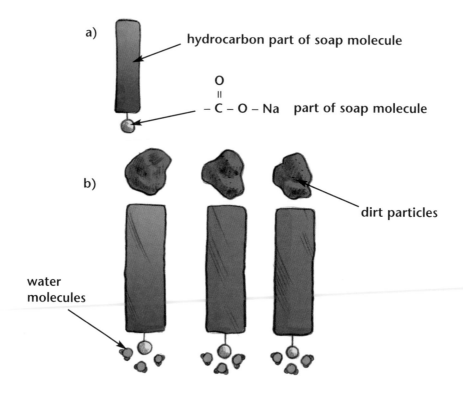

a) hydrocarbon part of soap molecule

$$\begin{array}{c} O \\ \| \\ -C-O-Na \end{array}$$ part of soap molecule

b) dirt particles

water molecules

Figure 16.

a) A soap molecule has a hydrocarbon end that is not soluble in water. Its other end is polar and attracts water molecules.

b) One end of a soap molecule attracts water. The other end attracts dirt and stains. As a result, soap brings dirt and water together so that the dirt can be washed away.

Detergents are similar to soap, but they are designed to penetrate stains better, are more soluble in cold water, and don't leave scumlike residues.

Making Suds

Procedure:

1. Use a straw to blow air softly into some soapy water. What happens?

2. Next, half fill a test tube or vial with water.

3. Cover the tube or vial and shake to mix the water with air. What do you see after shaking?

4. Now add a drop of liquid soap or detergent to the test tube or vial.

5. Cover the vessel and shake to mix the liquid with air.

Results and Conclusions

Try to explain why you find many small bubbles on the surface of the liquid when you stop shaking. Why weren't the bubbles there when you used water alone?

EXPERIMENT 3.5

Food Coloring, Water, Milk, and Soap

Question:

Does food coloring made from water and alcohol behave the same way when it is added to water or to milk?

Hypothesis:

No, food coloring is soluble in water, but not in milk.

Materials:

- cold water
- small plastic cup, such as a yogurt container
- food coloring
- cotton swab
- soapy water
- milk: whole, skim, 1 percent, 2 percent, powdered, cream, and half-and-half

Your grandparents may remember when milk came in clear bottles. At the top of the bottle would be the fatty part of the milk (the cream), which was less dense and more yellowish than the rest of the milk. People who liked cream in their coffee or tea would pour the liquid at the top of the bottle into a separate container.

You can still buy whole milk with the fat as it came from the cow. Normally, at least 3.25 percent of whole milk is fat. However, you don't see the cream. Through a process known as homogenization, the fatty part of the milk has been broken up into tiny particles to form a permanent emulsion. The milk is said to be homogenized. You can also buy skim milk, as well as 1 percent and 2 percent milk. The fat (cream) has been removed from skim milk. For 1 percent and 2 percent milk, the percentage refers to the fraction of the milk that is fat.

In this experiment you'll see how food coloring behaves in water and in milk of different fat concentrations. You'll also investigate the effect of soap on the behavior of food coloring in milk. The dyes in food coloring are dissolved in water and propylene glycol. As you may have guessed from the -ol ending, propylene glycol is an alcohol.

Procedure:

1. Pour some cold water into a small plastic cup such as an empty yogurt cup.

2. Add a drop of food coloring. Does the food coloring remain as a drop or does it spread through the water? Would you expect the food coloring to contain polar or nonpolar molecules? (Remember: polar molecules are usually soluble in one another.)

3. Pour out the water and food coloring.

4. Rinse the cup, then pour some whole milk into it.

5. Add a drop of the same food coloring you used before to the surface of the milk. What happens this time? How can you explain the difference in the behavior of the food coloring?

6. Dip one end of a cotton swab into some soapy water. Touch the edge of the food coloring on the milk with the soapy cotton swab.

Results and Conclusions

What happens? How can you explain what you observe? What happens if you add more soap to the milk?

Will the concentration of fat in the milk affect the way the food coloring responds to the milk and to soap? To find out, repeat the experiment using skim, 1 percent, 2 percent, and a powdered milk solution, as well as cream and half-and-half. What do you find?

 Science Project Ideas

- Investigate how cream is changed to butter. Then see if you can devise a way to make butter yourself.

- How would you expect the densities of the different concentrations of milk to compare? To check your predictions, obtain samples of skim, 1 percent, 2 percent, and whole milk, as well as cream. Measure the density of each sample. Do your results confirm your predictions?

- From the nutrition facts printed on milk containers, show that the concentration of fat in 1 percent milk really is one percent. Do the same for 2 percent and skim milk. What is the percentage of fat in whole milk? Why do you think it may differ for milk from different dairies?

EXPERIMENT 3.6

Cis-Trans Isomers

Question:

Can the properties of cis-trans isomers reveal which is the cis and which is the trans?

Hypothesis:

Solubility in water and pH are effective tests to identify cis and trans isomers.

Materials:

- safety gloves
- safety glasses
- balance
- maleic and fumaric acids (obtain from a school science lab or science supply company)
- paper
- water
- magnesium ribbon
- test tubes and test tube stoppers
- masking tape and marker
- graduated cylinder
- pH test paper (obtain from a school science lab or science supply company)
- calcium carbonate

Safety: *Wear gloves and safety glasses while doing this experiment.*

From Experiment 2.5, you know that isomers are compounds that have the same chemical formula but differ in how the atoms are arranged. In what is termed a *cis* arrangement of atoms, certain atoms or groups of atoms, such as OH, are on the same side of the molecule. In what is termed a *trans* arrangement, these groups are on opposite sides of the molecule. If a compound shows a cis isomer and a trans isomer, the compound is said to have cis-trans isomerism.

Figure 17a shows two carbon atoms joined by a double bond (four covalent electrons). Such a bond makes cis-trans isomers possible because the carbon atoms cannot rotate if they are joined by a double bond. In Figure 17b, you see the cis and trans forms of dichloroethene. In the cis isomer, as the drawings reveal, the two chlorine atoms are on the same side of the molecule. In the trans isomer arrangement, the two chlorine atoms are on opposite sides of the molecule. In this experiment you will examine two weak acids, maleic acid and fumaric acid. These two organic compounds are cis-trans isomers.

The two acids, shown in Figure 17c, have the same formula ($C_4H_4O_4$) but different physical properties because of their different structures. One is maleic acid, the other is fumaric acid. We have purposely not identified which acid is the trans arrangement and which is the cis arrangement. We leave that to you.

Figure 17.

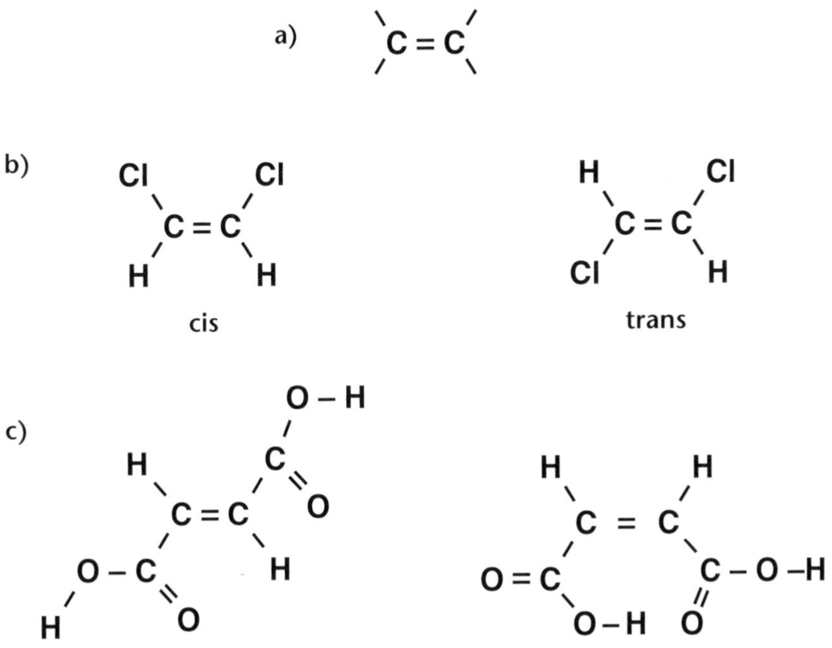

a) Here you see two carbon atoms joined by a double bond. The double bond prevents the joined atoms from rotating.
b) These two structural formulas show the cis and trans forms of dichloroethene.
c) Here you see structural formulas for the molecules of two organic acids. Both acids have the same formula, $C_4H_4O_4$, but different physical properties.

Procedure:

1. Weigh out 0.1 gram samples of maleic and fumaric acids on separate pieces of paper.

2. Label a test tube "M" for maleic acid; label a second test tube "F" for fumaric acid.

3. Add 10 mL of water to each tube. Pour each weighed sample into the appropriate labeled test tube.

4. Cover each tube with a stopper and shake. Which acid is more soluble in water? Which form, cis or trans, would you expect to be more polar? (Remember, polar molecules tend to be more soluble in water than are nonpolar molecules.)

5. Prepare another solution of maleic acid by dissolving 0.1 g of the acid in 20 mL of water. Divide the solution equally among three small test tubes.

6. To measure the pH (acidity) of the solution, insert a strip of pH test paper into one test tube. Compare the color of the strip with the colors on the test paper holder. What is the pH of the acid?

7. To a second sample of the acid, add a small piece of magnesium ribbon. What do you observe?

8. To the third sample, add a small piece of calcium carbonate. What do you observe? (Magnesium and calcium carbonate both react with hydrogen ions to form hydrogen gas.)

9. Repeat this experiment after dissolving 0.1 g of fumaric acid in 20 mL of water. How do the results with fumaric acid compare with those for maleic acid?

Results and Conclusions

Some properties of maleic and fumaric acids are shown in Table 2.

Based on the evidence from your experiment and the data in Table 2, which acid isomer do you think is the trans arrangement? Which is the cis arrangement? On what do you base your conclusion?

Table 2.

Some Properties of Maleic and Fumaric Acids

	maleic acid	fumaric acid
melting point (°C)	130.5	287
solubility in water (g/100mL at 25 °C)	79	0.7
approximate pH for 1g/200 mL of water	2	3

EXPERIMENT 3.7

Polymers and Diapers

Question:

Why is a polymer used in diapers?

Hypothesis:

The polymer sodium polyacrylate can absorb many times its weight in water.

Materials:

- **an adult**
- several superabsorbent diapers
- balance for weighing
- sink
- measuring cup
- water
- scissors
- forceps
- matches
- paper towel

Some organic molecules with a double or triple bond will join together to form long molecules that resemble a chain. The joining of like molecules to form heavier ones is called polymerization. The large molecules formed by this process are called polymers.

Figure 18a shows how two ethene (ethylene) molecules can be joined to form a molecule of butene. In Figure 18b you see that many ethene molecules can join to form a long-chain hydrocarbon.

There are many natural polymers such as starch, cellulose, fats, waxes, oils, and proteins (which include enzymes, hormones, wool, and silk). Manmade, or synthetic, polymers are found in plastics and textiles such as Lucite, Plexiglas, nylon, and polyester.

One synthetic polymer, sodium polyacrylate, is found in super-absorbent diapers.

Figure 18.

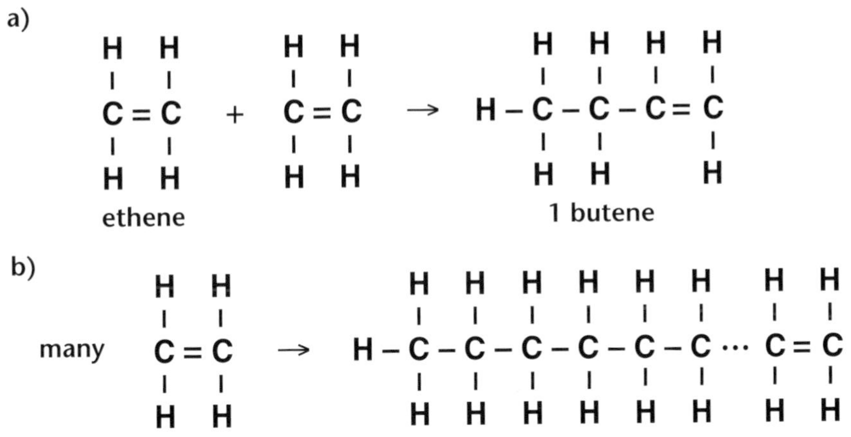

a)

$$
\begin{array}{ccc}
\underset{\text{ethene}}{\overset{\displaystyle H\ \ H}{\underset{\displaystyle H\ \ H}{\overset{|\quad|}{C=C}}}} & + & \overset{\displaystyle H\ \ H}{\underset{\displaystyle H\ \ H}{\overset{|\quad|}{C=C}}}
\end{array}
\;\rightarrow\;
\underset{\text{1 butene}}{
H-C-C-C=C
}
$$

H H   H H   H H H H
| | | | | | | |
C = C + C = C → H – C – C – C = C
| | | | | | |
H H   H H   H H   H
ethene   1 butene

b)

many   H H   H H H H H H   H H
| | | | | | | | | |
C = C → H – C – C – C – C – C – C ··· C = C
| | | | | | | | | |
H H   H H H H H H   H H

a) Like molecules with double or triple bonds can join to form larger molecules.

b) The joining of many of these small molecules can lead to very large molecules called polymers.

Procedure:

1. First remove one superabsorbent diaper from a package and weigh it.

2. Then place the diaper in a sink and open it. The polymer is enclosed within a thin rectangular cloth that runs along the center of the diaper.

3. Carefully pour a cup of water along the length of the central part of the diaper. What happens to the water? Continue to add cups of water until the diaper is saturated—which means it can hold no more water.

4. Lift the diaper and let any excess water fall into the sink.

5. Now reweigh the diaper. What weight of water was absorbed?

Results and Conclusions

How much water did one gram of the polymer absorb?

To find out, use scissors to carefully cut away the portion of a dry diaper that contains the polymer and weigh it. Then calculate the ratio:

$$\frac{\text{weight of water absorbed, in grams}}{\text{weight of polymer in grams}} = \text{water absorbed by 1 g of polymer}$$

To see what the polymer in a dry diaper looks like, use scissors to cut through the thin cloth that covers the sodium polyacrylate. What does the polymer look like? Describe its texture. Will it burn? To find out, use forceps to hold a sample of the polymer over a sink. **Ask an adult** to try to ignite the polymer with a match. Is the polymer flammable? What evidence do you have that polyacrylate is an organic compound? Remember that organic molecules contain carbon. Why are there warnings on diaper packages telling people not to allow diapered babies near flames?

To see what the polymer looks like after absorbing water, make a small slit in the saturated diaper. Describe the polymer after it has absorbed water. Is sodium polyacrylate hydrophilic or hydrophobic?

Do you think there should be warnings on superabsorbent diapers telling parents not to let babies wear such a diaper in a swimming pool?

Put a small sample of the wet polymer on a paper towel. Place the towel in a warm place. Does the wet polymer eventually dry? Does it return to its original form? If it does, will it still absorb water?

EXPERIMENT 3.8

Polymers and Plastics

Question:

Other than by appearance, color, and flexibility, how are plastics identified and distinguished from one another?

Hypothesis:

You can identify plastics by comparing their densities.

Materials:

- 6 different plastic food containers (coded 1, 2, 3, 4, 5, or 6 inside a small triangle on the bottom of most plastic containers)
- scissors
- envelopes or small containers
- marking pen
- block of wood
- ruler
- balance
- water
- steel objects such as washers, nuts, or bolts
- 100-mL graduated cylinder
- rubbing alcohol
- sugar
- spoon
- kosher salt

Plastics are formed by the polymerization of organic compounds. There are a number of common plastics that are used to package foods and liquids. Some of these include (1) polyethylene terephthalate (PET), (2) high-density polyethylene (HDPE), (3) polyvinyl chloride (PVC), (4) low-density polyethylene (LDPE), (5) polypropylene (PP), and (6) polystyrene (PS). The number preceding each plastic listed above is also the number used to code the plastic for recycling purposes.

Many communities ask residents to recycle plastics, and the code is useful in identifying the type of plastic. You will find the code number inside a small triangle on the bottom of most plastic containers.

Procedure:

1. To carry out this experiment you'll need to collect at least one container made from each of the plastics named above.

2. Once you've done that, use scissors to cut seven or more samples from each kind of plastic. The samples can be squares roughly about 2 cm (1 in) on a side.

3. Samples of each kind of plastic should be kept separate and placed in labeled envelopes or containers.

   Are there properties such as appearance, color, flexibility, response to bending, and texture that you can use to identify these plastics?

   One property that's very helpful in identifying substances is density. You found the density of water, cooking oil, and rubbing alcohol (70% isopropyl alcohol) in Experiment 3.3. You also found that liquids that are not miscible float on denser liquids and sink in less dense ones. The same is true of solids placed in liquids.

4. To confirm that solids sink in less dense liquids and float in denser ones, find a block of wood and measure its length, width, and height. How can you find its volume from these three measurements?

5. Next, weigh the block. Then calculate its density.

   Remember: density = weight ÷ volume.

6. Compare the density of the wood with the density of water, which is one gram per milliliter. Do you think the wood will sink or float in water? Place it in water. Were you right?

   Next, find the density of some steel objects such as washers, nuts, or bolts.

Procedure:

1. Gather a number of identical steel washers and weigh them.

2. Then carefully drop them into a 100-mL graduated cylinder that holds 50 mL of water. If the water rises to the 85-mL line, you'll know the volume of the washers is 35 mL (85 mL – 50 mL). Based on the way you measured the volume, would you expect the steel to be more or less dense than water?

3. Calculate the density of the steel. Were you right?

   It would be difficult to find the density of the different samples of plastic you've collected. They're too big to fit into a graduated cylinder. You might cut them into small pieces, weigh them, and put them in a graduated cylinder. But it would be difficult to submerge them in the cylinder if they float.

There is another way to find their approximate densities. You can place them in liquids whose density you know and see whether they sink or float. For example, if one plastic floats in water, you know its density is less than one gram per cubic centimeter. If another plastic sinks in water you know its density is greater than one gram per cubic centimeter. If you do this with a number of liquids with different densities, you can estimate the density of each plastic quite accurately.

You already know the density of water, cooking oil, and rubbing alcohol. You can also prepare some other liquids whose densities will be different from those of the three liquids you've already measured. Note that a milliliter and a cubic centimeter have the same volume.

Procedure:

Prepare each of the following liquids and measure their densities:

1. Mix 100 mL of rubbing alcohol with 40 mL of water.

2. Mix 100 mL of rubbing alcohol with 50 mL of water.

3. Add 140 mL of water to 70 grams of sugar and stir until the sugar dissolves.

4. Prepare a saturated solution of salt by adding 370 grams of kosher salt to one liter of water. Stir until no more salt will dissolve. It might be a good idea to leave this solution overnight to be sure as much salt as possible has dissolved. Some salt will remain undissolved.

5. Prepare a data table similar to Table 3. Test each sample by submerging the plastic in the liquid. Be sure to submerge it; surface tension might prevent it from sinking.

Table 3.

Finding the Approximate Density of Six Types of Plastics by Submerging Them in Liquids of Unknown Density

Liquid used	Approximate density of liquid	PLASTICS					
		1 (PET)	2 (HDPE)	3 (PVC)	4 (LDPE)	5 (PP)	6 (PS)
alcohol	see Experiment 3.3						
alcohol + water (100:40)							
alcohol + water (100:50)							
cooking oil	see Experiment 3.3						
water	1.0 g/cc						
sugar water							
salt water							

Results and Conclusions

In each of the liquids whose density you know, which plastics sink? Which float? In the blank spaces under each plastic, write an F or an S depending on whether the plastic floats or sinks in the liquid.

What's the approximate density of each type of plastic? Which plastic is the most dense? Which is the least dense?

 Science Project Idea

- Plexiglas is another plastic. Carry out an experiment to determine its density.

CHAPTER 4

Food:
Organic Compounds

Scientists divide the foods we eat into carbohydrates, fats, and proteins. All three types are organic compounds. Carbohydrates and fats contain only carbon, hydrogen, and oxygen. In addition to these elements, proteins contain nitrogen and sometimes sulfur, as well as phosphorus. Proteins are needed to make new cells and repair old ones. In order to use these basic food types to obtain energy, grow new tissue, and repair old tissue, we also need other essential nutrients—vitamins and minerals.

◀ For nourishment, we eat foods that are organic compounds. Vegetables are high in carbohydrates; the body needs other organic compounds as well, such as fats and proteins.

Carbohydrates

Carbohydrates are the most abundant and the least expensive type of food. The *carbo-* part of the term *carbohydrate* tells you that these compounds contain carbon. The Greek word for water is *hydor*. The *hydrate* part of carbohydrate indicates water (H_2O). The elements in carbohydrates are chemically combined in a particular ratio. Carbohydrate molecules contain two hydrogen atoms for every oxygen atom.

Sugars are carbohydrates. The Greek word for sugar is *sakcharon*. There are simple sugars, such as glucose and fructose, which are called monosaccharides. All monosaccharide molecules have 6 carbon atoms, 12 hydrogen atoms, and 6 oxygen atoms ($C_6H_{12}O_6$). The properties of these simple sugars may differ because the atoms in their compounds have different arrangements (see Figures 19a and 19b).

Disaccharide sugars ($C_{12}H_{22}O_{11}$)—sucrose, lactose, and maltose—occur in nature. They can be converted to monosaccharide sugars by reactions that add a molecule of water. Disaccharides must be converted (digested) to monosaccharides in your body before they can be absorbed into your blood.

Polysaccharides, such as starch, are polymers made by the union of many monosaccharide molecules. The formula for a starch, $(C_6H_{10}O_5)_n$, reveals that each of the monosaccharide molecules must lose a molecule of water as the polymer is formed. Again, the starch we eat must be digested and changed to monosaccharides before it can be used by our body cells.

Figure 19.

a)

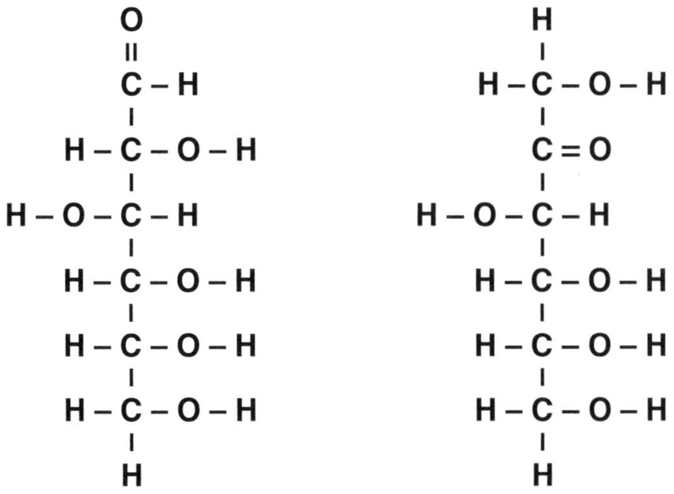

glucose	fructose
O ‖ C – H | H – C – O – H | H – O – C – H | H – C – O – H | H – C – O – H | H – C – O – H | H	H | H – C – O – H | C = O | H – O – C – H | H – C – O – H | H – C – O – H | H – C – O – H | H

b) $C_{12}H_{22}O_{11} + H_2O \rightarrow C_6H_{12}O_6 + C_6H_{12}O_6$

a) Glucose and fructose are both monosaccharides, $C_6H_{12}O_6$, but their atoms are arranged differently, as you can see from these structural formulas.

b) Disaccharide sugars, such as sucrose, can be converted to monosaccharide sugars by hydrolysis (combining chemically with water).

EXPERIMENT 4.1

Testing for Carbohydrates

Question:
How can you easily identify a carbohydrate?

Hypothesis:
Some carbohydrates can be identified by how certain chemicals make them change color.

Materials:

- plastic gloves
- safety glasses
- tincture of iodine
- eyedropper
- water
- small, clear drinking glass
- cornstarch
- saucers
- raw and cooked potatoes
- white bread
- milk
- white meat, such as chicken breast
- unsalted crackers
- Diastix® reagent sticks (from a drugstore)
- corn or maple syrup
- graduated cylinder
- toothpick
- sucrose (table sugar)
- variety of juices, such as grape juice, orange juice, apple juice, etc.
- teaspoon

Testing for Starch (Polysaccharide)

Safety: *To avoid staining your fingers and to protect your eyes, wear plastic gloves and safety glasses while doing this experiment.*

Starch can be identified very easily because it turns dark blue in the presence of iodine. Furthermore, when starch is slowly converted into sugar, samples change color from dark blue to bluish red, to red, to faint red, to no change.

Procedure:

1. Prepare a dilute iodine solution by mixing about 10 drops of tincture of iodine with 30 drops of water in a small, clear drinking glass. **Safety:** *Be careful handling iodine. It's a poison.*

2. To confirm the test for starch, place a small amount of cornstarch on a saucer.

3. Add a drop of the iodine solution. What do you observe?

4. In separate shallow dishes, place a slice of crushed raw potato, some cooked potato, a piece of white bread, some milk, some chopped white meat such as chicken breast, and an unsalted cracker.

5. Test each sample by adding a drop of the iodine solution. Record your results in a notebook. **Safety:** *Do not put anything with iodine on it into your mouth!*

6. When you finish the experiment, discard the food samples and wash the dishes they were on.

Results and Conclusions

Which foods contain starch? What other foods might you test for starch?

Testing for a Simple Sugar (Monosaccharide)

Diastix® reagent sticks are used by diabetics to test for sugar in their urine. These sticks are plastic strips with a chemical at one end. The chemical turns color in the presence of glucose and can measure the concentration of the sugar in a solution. You can obtain such strips, or a suitable substitute, from a drugstore.

Procedure:

1. Pour about 5 mL of corn syrup or maple syrup into a saucer. Add about 5 mL of water and dip the chemical end of a reagent stick in the liquid. Follow the directions on the bottle of the sticks to test for glucose. Does the syrup contain glucose? From the test stick, can you determine the concentration of glucose in the syrup?

2. Repeat the experiment using 10 mL of a saturated solution of sucrose (table sugar). Does this sugar solution contain any glucose?

3. In separate dishes, place a few milliliters of milk and a variety of juices, such as grape juice, orange juice, apple juice, and so on. Test with a reagent stick. Do any of these liquids contain glucose?

4. Next, crush or pour samples of raw and cooked potatoes, an unsalted cracker, bread, milk, and cooked white chicken meat onto separate saucers. Add about a teaspoon of warm water to each sample and stir. Then use a reagent stick to test for glucose. What do you conclude?

5. Chew an unsalted cracker for two or three minutes so that it has time to react with the saliva in your mouth. As you chew, you may notice that the cracker begins to have a sweet taste. Saliva contains amylase, an enzyme that breaks starch into sucrose, which is what you may taste. Can it break the disaccharide into glucose, a monosaccharide?

6. To find out, after you've thoroughly chewed the unsalted cracker spit out two samples onto separate saucers. Mix each of these samples with a little water. Test one sample with a drop of iodine solution. Test the second sample with a reagent stick. Did the thoroughly chewed cracker still contain starch? Did it contain any glucose?

7. Mix ¼ teaspoon of cornstarch with an equal amount of corn or maple syrup, which, as you know from an earlier test, contains a simple sugar. Add a teaspoon of water and stir the mixture with a toothpick. Pour a small amount of the mixture onto a saucer and test with a reagent stick.

8. Add a drop of iodine solution to the mixture. **Safety:** *Remember that iodine is poisonous!*

Results and Conclusions

Can you get a positive test for glucose when the sugar is mixed with starch? Can you get a positive test for starch when the starch is mixed with glucose?

Can Diastix® reagent sticks be used to test for other simple sugars such as fructose, galactose, and mannose? Design and carry out an experiment to find out.

 Science Project Ideas

- Sometimes starch is used in medicinal pills to bind other solids together. Do you think aspirin tablets contain starch? Design and conduct an experiment to find out.

- Do some research to find out how chemists test for disaccharides such as sucrose, lactose, and maltose.

EXPERIMENT 4.2

Heating Carbohydrates

Question:
What happens if you heat a carbohydrate?

Hypothesis:
The carbohydrate will be decomposed into simpler substances.

Materials:

- **an adult**
- heavy-duty aluminum foil
- safety glasses
- oven mitt
- clothespin
- sugar
- candle and candleholder
- matches
- a friend
- cooking pan
- cold water
- cornstarch
- strips of blue cobalt chloride paper
- carbohydrate-rich foods such as flour, bread, raw potato, corn syrup
- gelatin powder
- sink
- teaspoon
- measuring cup
- watercolor paintbrush
- file card
- tongs

Procedure:

1. Make a number of small pans with handles by folding pieces of heavy-duty aluminum foil as shown in Figure 20a. **Safety:** *Put on safety glasses and an oven mitt to protect your eyes and hand.* Then use a clothes-pin to grasp the handle of one of the pans.

2. Place a small amount of ordinary sugar (sucrose) in the pan.

3. Under **adult supervision**, put a candle in a candleholder. Light the candle and heat the sugar by holding the pan above the candle flame as shown in Figure 20b.

Figure 20.

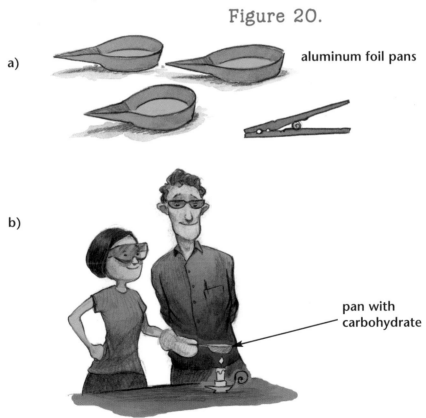

a)   aluminum foil pans

b)

pan with
carbohydrate

a) You can make small pans by folding pieces of heavy-duty aluminum foil.
b) Under **adult supervision**, use a clothespin to hold a small pan with a small amount of carbohydrate in it over a candle flame.

Results and Conclusions

What happens to the sugar when you heat it? Is there any evidence of vapor coming from the decomposing sugar? If there is, ask a friend to hold a cooking pan of cold water in the vapor. Does any liquid condense on the bottom of the pan? If it does, what do you think that liquid might be?

If you can obtain strips of blue cobalt chloride paper, place the end of a strip in the condensed liquid.

Cobalt chloride paper turns pink in water. Can you identify the liquid now?

Did the sugar change? Did it turn black? If it did, what do you think the black substance is? (For the answer, see page 156.)

Procedure:

1. Repeat the experiment, this time with a very small amount of cornstarch in place of the sugar. What happens to the cornstarch when you heat it?

2. Try heating very small amounts of other carbohydrates and carbohydrate-rich foods such as flour, bread, raw potato, and a drop of corn syrup.

Results and Conclusions

What seems to be the common substance that remains after all these carbohydrates are heated? What else do you think is produced when these carbohydrates decompose? If you had cobalt chloride strips, you know the answer.

Do other foods behave in the same way? To find out, you might try heating a protein such as gelatin powder. Does the gelatin powder decompose like a carbohydrate when heated?

Another Invisible Ink

Decomposing a carbohydrate by heating can be the basis for an invisible ink. **Safety:** *Do this experiment near a sink under adult supervision. Should the card you will use start to burn during the experiment, drop it in the sink and turn on the water.*

Procedure:

1. To make such an ink, dissolve one teaspoon of sugar in ¼ cup of hot water. Use a watercolor paintbrush as a "pen" and the sugar solution as "invisible ink."

2. Using your pen and invisible ink, write a short message on a file card.

3. After the invisible ink has dried, under **adult supervision**, carefully heat the paper by holding it with tongs above a candle flame.

Results and Conclusions

Why does the message slowly appear?

EXPERIMENT 4.3

Testing for Fat in Food

Question:

Is there a simple test for identifying most fatty foods?

Hypothesis:

Most fatty foods will leave a translucent stain when rubbed on brown paper.

Materials:

- brown paper bag
- cooking oil
- water
- bacon
- hot dog
- peanut butter
- French fries
- butter
- margarine
- lard
- milk
- a walnut
- cream
- orange juice
- lemonade
- mayonnaise
- low-fat mayonnaise
- egg white
- egg yolk

Fats: An Energy Source and a Way to Store It

Carbohydrates make up the bulk of the food most people consume. They also provide most of the energy our bodies need. However, we cannot live for long on a diet of only carbohydrates. We need protein to provide the matter used for growth and for the repair of cells.

Enzymes that help digest food and regulate other chemical processes that take place within our bodies are also proteins. And we require a variety of minerals such as calcium, iron, magnesium, potassium, iodine, zinc, and others.

We also need some fat to make adipose tissue, the soft tissue that insulates our bodies and cushions our internal organs. And we need fats to carry certain fat-soluble vitamins to our cells. Both fat-soluble and water-soluble vitamins are needed to regulate the many chemical reactions that go on within our bodies and make life possible.

Fats and oils (liquid fat) contain carbon, hydrogen, and oxygen, but not in the same ratio as carbohydrates. If you've ever eaten overcooked bacon, you're aware that fat contains carbon, the black substance that remains after fat has been decomposed by heating. Fats contain more carbon and hydrogen but less oxygen per gram than carbohydrates. They also provide twice as much energy per gram as do carbohydrates or proteins.

If you eat more food than your body needs, the excess is stored as fat in cells that make up adipose tissue. Everyone has some adipose tissue beneath their skin as well as on and in internal organs such as the kidneys and intestines. The fat is a storehouse of energy.

Following is a simple test that can be used to identify many fatty foods.

Procedure:

1. Tear off one side of a brown paper bag.

2. Put a drop of cooking oil on your finger and rub it in a circular fashion on one small section of the brown paper.

3. Use another finger to rub some water into another section of the paper in the same way.

4. If you hold the paper up to the light, you'll see that the spot made with the cooking oil and, perhaps, the one made with water are translucent—they transmit light.

Results and Conclusions

The liquids transmit light because they fill in the spaces between the wood fibers in the paper that trap the light. The water spot will become opaque as the liquid evaporates, but the oily spot, which contains fat, will remain translucent. Why do you think the oily spot remains translucent?

Hint: *Does oil evaporate quickly?*

Try testing some other substances. Make circles in the brown paper by rubbing on it some uncooked bacon and a cross-section of an uncooked hot dog. Try some peanut butter, French fries, ordinary butter, margarine, and lard. Also try milk, a walnut, cream, orange juice, lemonade, mayonnaise, low-fat mayonnaise, egg white, and egg yolk. Which of these substances give a positive test for fat? Which appear to have little or no fat?

Safety: *Be sure to wash your hands after handling raw meat or eggs.*

EXPERIMENT 4.4

Testing for Proteins

Question:

How can you test for the presence of proteins in a water solution?

Hypothesis:

One way is to add certain chemicals that cause a change in the solution's color if protein is present; another is that a beam of light passing through the solution will reflect off any protein molecules that are present.

Materials:

- **an adult**
- safety glasses
- rubber gloves
- balance
- sodium hydroxide (NaOH) crystals (from school science laboratory)
- copper sulfate ($CuSO_4$·$5H_2O$) crystals (from school science laboratory)
- cold water
- eggs
- large test tube
- stopper

(continued)

(continued)

- spoon (for stirring)
- eyedropper
- flour
- gelatin
- potato
- bread
- milk
- cooked white meat of chicken
- crackers
- sugar
- teaspoon
- small glass or beaker
- warm water
- cup
- small test tube
- glass of water
- dark room
- penlight or small flashlight

Proteins can be identified by the Biuret test. Because this test involves the use of sodium hydroxide (lye) solution, which is harmful to skin and eyes, you will need **an adult** to help you with this experiment. **Safety:** *You should both wear safety glasses and rubber gloves throughout the experiment.*

Procedure:

1. **The adult** can prepare the sodium hydroxide (NaOH) solution by adding 10 g of the white solid to 100 g of cold water and stirring until the solid is dissolved.

2. While **the adult** is preparing the sodium hydroxide solution, you can prepare a 3 percent solution of copper sulfate by adding 3 g of blue copper sulfate ($CuSO_4 \cdot 5H_2O$) crystals to 100 mL of water.

Egg white from a raw egg is a good source of protein. It can be used to demonstrate a positive test for protein.

3. Separate the white of an egg from its yolk as you did in Experiment 3.3. When most of the white has been removed, discard the yolk, which is primarily fat, or save it for cooking. **Safety:** *Always wash your hands after handling raw eggs!*

4. Pour the egg white into a large test tube or a small jar or bottle. Add an equal volume of water and stopper the tube or bottle. Be sure the stopper seals the tube or bottle completely! Shake the jar thoroughly to mix the egg white and water.

5. Have **the adult** add a volume of the sodium hydroxide solution equal to the volume of mixture of egg white and water. Then stopper and shake the tube again.

6. Next, add about 5 drops of the copper sulfate solution, stopper, and shake once more.

Results and Conclusions

A violet or blue-violet color indicates the presence of protein. The darker the color, the greater the concentration of protein.

Mash samples of different foods separately in water. You might use flour, gelatin, pieces of potato, bread, milk, cooked white meat of chicken, crackers, and sugar. **Ask the adult** to help you test these foods for protein. Which foods give a positive test for protein? Which foods can you conclude do not contain protein?

Proteins and John Tyndall

Irish physicist John Tyndall (1820–1893) discovered that if a beam of light passes through water or any clear liquid containing small molecules, the beam cannot be seen from the side of the clear vessel holding the liquid. Larger particles, however, do reflect some of the light, making the beam visible, just as a beam of sunlight can be seen when it shines through dust particles in a room.

Procedure:

1. To observe what Tyndall saw, pour a teaspoon of sugar into a small glass or beaker. Fill the vessel about halfway with warm water and stir the mixture with a spoon. As you can see, the sugar dissolves in the water to form a clear solution.

2. Next, separate the white of an egg from the yolk as described earlier. Use an eyedropper to transfer the egg white to a small test tube. **Safety:** *Again, always wash your hands after handling raw eggs!*

3. Take both liquids and a glass of water to a dark area. Use a penlight or a small flashlight to shine a narrow beam of light through the sugar solution while you view the liquid from the side, as shown in Figure 21.

Results and Conclusions

If you can see the beam in the liquid when you view it from the side, you're observing what is known as the Tyndall effect.

Is there a Tyndall effect when you shine the light through the sugar solution? Is there a Tyndall effect when you shine the light through a glass of water?

Remembering that protein molecules, such as those found in egg white, are some of the largest molecules known, would you expect to observe the Tyndall effect when you shine the light through the egg white? Try it. Was your prediction correct?

Figure 21.

clear container

Can you see the beam of light from the side? If you can, you are observing the Tyndall effect.

EXPERIMENT 4.5

A Catalyst for the Reaction of an Organic Compound

Question:

Can a catalyst speed up the rate at which sugar is burned?

Hypothesis:

Yes, catalysts make sugar oxidize (burn) faster.

Materials:

- **an adult**
- sugar (sucrose) cube
- forceps
- a sink
- matches
- wood ashes

As you saw in the first chapter, a chemical reaction is a process in which one or more substances change to form new substances. A catalyst is a substance that changes the rate of a chemical reaction without being changed itself. Your saliva and the enzymes in your stomach and intestines serve as catalysts in the digestion of your food. They accelerate the change of starch and disaccharide sugars to monosaccharides, proteins to amino acids, and fats to fatty acids and glycerol. The smaller molecules formed during the digestion process can pass through the intestinal walls and into the bloodstream. In this experiment you'll see how a catalyst can increase the rate at which ordinary sugar, sucrose, is oxidized (burned).

Procedure:

1. Using forceps, hold one end of a sugar cube over a sink. **Ask an adult** to bring a burning match near the other end of the cube in an effort to make the sugar burn. The sugar may melt, but it's not likely that it will burn.

2. Next, smear the end of the sugar cube with wood ashes. You can obtain wood ashes from a fireplace or **ask an adult** to burn some wooden matches or toothpicks.

3. Again, **ask the adult** to try to ignite the ash-coated end of the sugar cube as you hold it over a sink.

Results and Conclusions

What happens this time? How have the wood ashes affected the rate at which the sugar oxidizes? Can you identify at least one of the products formed when sugar burns? If so, what is it?

 Science Project Ideas

- Do some research to find out what enzymes in the digestive system catalyze the digestion of carbohydrates. Where are these enzymes produced? If possible, obtain these enzymes in powdered form. Use them to show that polysaccharides and disaccharides are converted to glucose during digestion.

- Bile, a substance secreted by the liver, is found in the small intestine. What role does bile play in the digestion of fats? Design an experiment to show how bile acts on fats.

CHAPTER 5

Baking: Organic Chemistry in the Kitchen

The food we eat is made up of organic compounds. From ancient times the preparation of many foods has involved baking. To bake food we surround it with heat, and often we use a chemical or biological agent to make the food rise (expand) as it's heated. In this chapter you'll explore some of the ways baking demonstrates organic chemistry in action.

A batter can be made to rise in many different ways. You probably know that yeast is used to make

◀ Popovers rise (expand) with the help of air and steam rather than yeast, baking powder, or baking soda.

most breads rise, but do you know how it works? What about muffins, cakes, cream puffs, and popovers? Yeast isn't used in them, but still they rise when baked.

Substances that make a batter rise are called leavening agents. The leavening agents used most often in cooking are yeast, baking soda, and baking powder. A gas such as carbon dioxide, air, or steam must be trapped in a flour mixture. When the mixture is heated, the gas will expand, causing the mixture to rise.

EXPERIMENT 5.1

Making Popovers: Using Air and Steam as Leavening Agents

Question:

Can baked goods rise without a leavening agent?

Hypothesis:

Yes. The heat from the oven turns water in the popover dough to steam, a gas that promotes rising.

Materials:

- **an adult**
- oven
- 8 muffin cups
- bowl
- 2 eggs
- fork
- measuring cup
- 1 cup milk
- 1 cup all-purpose flour
- table salt
- teaspoon
- butter to grease muffin cups
- potholder

Procedure:

1. **Ask an adult** to preheat an oven to 450°F.

2. Grease eight muffin cups with butter.

3. Break two eggs into a bowl; discard the shells. Beat the eggs vigorously with a fork.

4. Continue to beat while adding 1 cup of milk, 1 cup of all-purpose flour, and 1 teaspoon of salt. Beat until the batter is smooth. Don't over-beat!

5. Fill the muffin cups with the batter you've beaten. Wash your hands thoroughly.

6. Bake the popovers for 25 minutes, then lower the temperature to 350°F and bake 15 to 20 minutes longer until golden brown. Try not to open the oven during the cooking time. If your oven has an oven light, use it to check on the popovers' progress.

7. **Ask an adult** to remove the popovers from the oven.

Results and Conclusions

After the popovers have cooled slightly, break one open. They should be filled with air and almost hollow inside. Can you explain why? Remember, in the recipe you were beating eggs with milk. Both have high water content, which, when heated, becomes steam.

 Science Project Idea

- There are many variables you can change in a popover recipe—the ingredients, oven temperature, mixing technique, cooking time, etc. Try some of the following changes to the recipe to see what happens: (1) Don't beat the eggs before adding the other ingredients. Will the popovers still rise? Will they rise as much? Will there be any change in the texture or consistency? (2) What will happen if you don't preheat the oven? Will they still rise? (3) Can you use low-fat milk, soy milk, or coconut milk? (4) What will happen if you use an egg substitute product? (5) The original recipe says not to over-beat. What happens if you do?

EXPERIMENT 5.2

Baking Soda as a Leavening Agent

Question:

Why is baking soda such an effective leavening agent?

Hypothesis:

Baking soda is a base and produces a gas when mixed with an acid.

Materials:

- **an adult**
- old teaspoon
- baking soda
- saucer
- water
- stove
- pan for boiling water
- vinegar
- lemon juice

In this experiment we'll try baking soda as a leavening agent. We want it to produce a gas that will make a batter rise. Should the baking soda be mixed with a liquid? Is heat needed?

Procedure:

1. To find out, place one teaspoon of baking soda on a saucer and add one teaspoon of cold water. Is any gas produced?

2. Repeat the experiment, but this time **ask an adult** to add one teaspoon of boiling water to the baking soda. Is any gas produced?

3. Next, add one teaspoon of vinegar to the baking soda. What happens? Is a gas produced?

Results and Conclusions

Baking soda ($NaHCO_3$) is a chemical compound also known as sodium bicarbonate. If you did Experiment 1.2 using red cabbage juice as a pH indicator, you know that baking soda is a base. To make it work as a leavening agent, you need to produce some type of gas. Vinegar is a solution of acetic acid (CH_3COOH). A chemical reaction occurs when mixing an acid with a base. In this case, the gas produced is carbon dioxide. The reaction can be written:

$$NaHCO_3 + CH_3COOH \longrightarrow NaCH_3COO + H_2O + CO_2$$

That is, sodium bicarbonate plus acetic acid produces sodium acetate plus water plus carbon dioxide.

Try adding some lemon juice to the baking soda. Lemon juice contains citric acid. Is a gas produced?

As you've seen, lemon juice as well as vinegar can produce carbon dioxide from baking soda. In fact, many acids will have the same effect.

Look at recipes in a cookbook that call for baking soda as the leavening agent. Can you identify the acid that will react with the baking soda?

EXPERIMENT 5.3

Baking Powder as a Leavening Agent

Question:

Why do some recipes use baking soda as the leavening agent and some use baking powder?

Hypothesis:

One reason is that baking soda is basic and will taste bitter unless an acidic ingredient is added, while baking power is neutral in taste.

Materials:

- **an adult**
- double-acting baking powder
- teaspoon
- water
- saucer
- boiling water

Have you ever wondered why some recipes call for baking soda and some call for baking powder? Is there a major difference or can they be substituted for each other in a recipe?

Procedure:

1. To find out, begin by adding one teaspoon of baking powder to a saucer. Then add one teaspoon of cold water to the baking powder. Is a gas produced?

2. Repeat the experiment, but this time **ask an adult** to add one tea-spoon of boiling water to the baking powder. What happens?

Results and Conclusions

In both cases, you should have seen a surge of bubbles from a gas being released in a chemical reaction. The gas being released is carbon dioxide. You probably witnessed two different chemical reactions happening at the different temperatures.

A major difference between baking soda and baking powder is that baking soda (sodium bicarbonate) is basic and will result in a bitter taste unless the recipe contains an acidic ingredient to neutralize the bitterness. Meanwhile, baking powder is a mixture of baking soda and powdered acids—an acid and a base. This combination makes baking powder neutral, so it doesn't much affect the taste.

Further, baking soda begins to react as soon as the mixture is made and must be baked immediately, while most baking powder can stand a while before being baked. Dry cornstarch is added to baking powder to absorb moisture to further insure it doesn't start reacting before it should.

Double-acting baking powder is often used in recipes. There are two reactions that can occur with double-acting baking powder because there are two different acids in it. The first reaction occurs when water is added to it. Many carbon dioxide bubbles develop. When heat is added, another reaction takes place. The acid that reacts with water is usually cream of tartar ($KHC_4H_4O_6$). It can also be tartaric acid ($C_4H_6O_6$) or monocalcium phosphate ($CaHPO_4$). The acid in baking powder that reacts to heat is usually aluminum sulfate ($Al_2[SO_4]_3$).

Look at the ingredients listed on your container of double-acting baking powder. What acids does it contain?

EXPERIMENT 5.4

The Same Recipe Using Different Leavening Agents

Question:
Can you change a recipe to use either baking soda or baking powder when the recipe calls for the other?

Hypothesis:
Yes, but you'll have to carefully account for their different strengths as leavening agents.

Materials:
- **an adult**
- mixing bowl
- measuring cup
- mixing spoon
- biscuit cutter
- waxed paper
- rolling pin
- baking sheet
- oven

For baking powder biscuits:
- 2 cups flour
- 1 teaspoon salt

- 4 teaspoons baking powder
- $1/3$ cup vegetable oil
- $2/3$ cup of whole milk

For baking soda biscuits:
- 2 cups flour
- 1 teaspoon baking soda
- 1 teaspoon salt
- $1/3$ cup vegetable oil
- $2/3$ cup buttermilk

Now that you've discovered the difference between baking soda and baking powder, you should also know that baking soda is about four times stronger as a leavening agent than baking powder. In other words, if a recipe calls for 1 teaspoon of baking soda and you wanted to use baking powder, you'd need to use 4 teaspoons of baking powder.

Try out the two basic recipes for the biscuits as listed above. Note the changes for the two leavening agents. See if you notice any differences in the resulting biscuits. Try to follow the procedures for the two recipes in the same way and in the same amount of time for the different leavening agents so that those factors don't become possible variables. A great way to insure that these factors stay constant would be to have someone else follow one recipe as you make the other. Then you could cook both sets of biscuits at the same time!

Procedure:

1. **Ask an adult** to preheat the oven to 450°F.

2. Mix dry ingredients together in a bowl. Pour milk and oil into a cup but don't mix.

3. Pour the liquids into the dry ingredients. Mix until the dough forms a ball.

4. Put the dough on a sheet of waxed paper that is double the size of the dough. Put the dough near the edge of one side of the paper.

5. Lift the other side of the waxed paper over the dough and knead by pressing down on the dough through the waxed paper with the heel of your hand. Turn and repeat this process until the dough is smooth.

6. Roll the dough to ½-inch thickness with the rolling pin, keeping a piece of waxed paper between the dough and rolling pin.

7. Cut out biscuits with a biscuit cutter or the rim of a glass with approximately a 1½-inch diameter and place the biscuits on a baking sheet.

8. Bake for 10 to 12 minutes until golden brown. Each recipe makes about 16 biscuits.

Results and Conclusions

Compare the biscuits. How well did they rise? Is their texture the same? Did one take longer to cook than the other? Do they taste the same? If there are differences, what may have caused them?

Do you know why you had to use buttermilk instead of whole milk in the baking soda biscuits? Could you use buttermilk in the baking powder biscuits and get the same results as you got using whole milk?

When you've finished your comparison, invite people to help you eat the biscuits. You might cut up strawberries, add whipped cream, and make individual strawberry shortcakes!

 Science Project Ideas

- Design and carry out an experiment to show that one part of baking soda is equivalent to approximately four parts of baking powder as a leavening agent.

- Try preparing other recipes using baking soda and baking powder as leavening agents. Make other substitutions as needed.

- Test the pH of soy milk and coconut milk. Can either of them be used with baking soda as a substitute for baking powder?

EXPERIMENT 5.5

Yeast as a Leavening Agent

Question:

What is the chemical process behind yeast as a leavening agent?

Hypothesis:

The enzymes in yeast change sugar to carbon dioxide gas and alcohol.

Materials:

- package of dry yeast or a cake of compressed yeast
- warm water 27–38°C (80–100°F)
- 4 glasses
- tablespoon
- table sugar
- corn syrup
- flour
- measuring cup
- thermometer
- paper labels
- a pen
- clock

Yeast is a living organism, a single-celled fungus named *Saccharomyces cerevisiae*. It's a very distant cousin of mushrooms. Yeast feeds on sugar, which is then converted to alcohol and carbon dioxide.

Procedure:

1. Mix some yeast with warm water and table sugar (sucrose). Remember, yeast is a living organism. Don't use hot water. If the water is too hot, you'll kill the cells. The temperature range that is best for yeast to become active is between 27 and 38°C (80 and 100°F). If the water is too cold, the yeast will stay inactive or the reaction will be very slow.

Results and Conclusions

When you mix the yeast with the warm water and sugar, you should detect an odor as the yeast enzymes convert the sugar to carbon dioxide and alcohol. You should be able to smell the alcohol. The chemical equation for this process is

$$\text{yeast enzymes} + \underset{\text{sucrose}}{C_{12}H_{22}O_{11}} + \underset{\text{water}}{H_2O} \longrightarrow \underset{\text{alcohol}}{4C_2H_5OH} + \underset{\substack{\text{carbon}\\\text{dioxide}}}{4CO_2}$$

Can you detect bubbles of carbon dioxide?

Does yeast have a favorite carbohydrate, or does one type of carbohydrate react faster with yeast than others?

You learned in Chapter 4 that starch is made of long chains of monosaccharide sugar molecules linked together. Can yeast convert starch to alcohol and carbon dioxide?

Procedure:

1. To explore the qualities of yeast, you'll need warm water. Check the temperature of the water from your faucet with a thermometer. If you can get water from your faucet at temperatures of 27–38°C, you shouldn't have to heat the water.

2. Put ⅔ cup of warm water into each of four glasses. Label the glasses: sugar, corn syrup, flour, water only.

3. Put two tablespoons of table sugar in one glass, the same amount of corn syrup in another glass, and the same amount of flour in the third glass. Add nothing to the water in the fourth glass.

4. Place an equal amount of yeast (about ½ teaspoon) in each glass. Don't mix.

5. Observe all four glasses immediately after adding the yeast, then after 10 minutes, after 20 minutes, and after 30 minutes. Look for bubbles of gas and check for odor.

Results and Conclusions

In which glass did you first observe bubbles? Did you detect any odor? Did one produce bubbles continuously? Did they all eventually produce bubbles, indicating that the yeast was converting the carbohydrate into carbon dioxide and alcohol? Why did you add only water and yeast to the fourth glass?

Baking yeast uses glucose as its main food source. Can you guess which of the carbohydrates you used has the most glucose in it?

 Science Project Ideas

- Many types of sugars and starches are used in baking. Try this same experiment with other sugar sources such as honey, brown sugar, and molasses. Do the same with different starches, such as different kinds of flour and cornstarch.

- Is there a limit to how much sugar yeast can digest? Can too much sugar inhibit the leavening process?

EXPERIMENT 5.6

Testing Flours for Gluten Content

Question:

How do all-purpose flour, cake flour, and bread flour compare?

Hypothesis:

These three flours have different amounts of protein. The dough made with them will differ in elasticity, size, and color.

Materials:

- **an adult**
- oven mitt
- 3 labeled bowls
- all-purpose flour
- cake flour
- bread flour
- clock or watch
- measuring cup
- cool water
- 3 spoons
- cookie sheet
- room-temperature water
- oven
- balance (if available)

Wheat flour provides the structure for most baked goods. Flour is made from grain that's compressed in its processing, releasing starches and proteins. When liquids are added to wheat flour and kneaded, two proteins in the flour, gliadin and glutenin, combine to form gluten. Gluten is a tough, elastic material. When dough is cooked, the gluten stretches and traps the gas bubbles, causing the dough to rise.

Different flours have different amounts of protein. Flours with high protein content will be able to make more gluten and thus a stronger dough. Flour with less protein and, thus, more starch will make a more delicate, tender dough.

Procedure:

1. Label three bowls with three types of flour: all-purpose flour, cake flour, and bread flour.

2. Place 1 cup of each different flour in each bowl.

   Add ½ cup of room-temperature water to each bowl.

3. Mix the water and flour in the bowls with separate spoons. Then knead each mixture until it forms a rubbery, soft dough.

4. Put each dough back into its proper bowl. Add enough cool water to each bowl to cover the dough. After ten minutes, pour off the white liquid that has formed and add fresh water. Make sure the dough doesn't fall apart. Squeeze it into a ball each time you change the water, rinsing off your hands between bowls.

5. Follow this procedure at ten-minute intervals for an hour.

6. Carefully observe the three batches of dough after an hour. Look for any differences in elasticity, size, and color. Continue to change the water for each dough until the water is no longer white. Some types of dough may take longer. Once all the batches are leaving the water almost clear, make careful observations again.

7. While you're making your observations, **ask an adult** to preheat an oven to 450°F.

8. Using an oven mitt, **an adult** should place the three batches of dough on a cookie sheet in the oven for 15 to 30 minutes.

9. Remove the dough batches. Observe any changes in size. Let them cool.

Results and Conclusions

Compare their weights by lifting two at a time with opposite hands or by weighing them on a balance. Which dough is heaviest? Which of the three doughs is lightest?

What do you think washed away in the water? Do you think it might be the starch in the flour or the protein? Which type of flour do you think has the most protein? Which flour has the most starch? Which flour was the most elastic?

 ## Science Project Ideas

- Wheat flour is the source of gluten. Some type of wheat flour is called for in most recipes for bread and muffins, even in recipes for corn muffins or rye bread. With an adult's help, repeat Experiment 5.6 using some flours you haven't tested, including whole wheat flour.

- Find a recipe for muffins. With an adult's help, in one batch use all-purpose flour; in another batch use cake flour (be sure it's not self-rising). Do you detect any difference in the muffins?

- Design and carry out experiments to test other variables that might affect the formation of gluten, such as how long you beat the batter, how much water is added, and so on.

Answers

p. 52.
$${}^{12}_{6}C$$

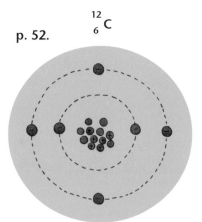

$${}^{13}_{6}C$$ will have 7 neutrons, 6 protons, and 6 electrons.

$${}^{14}_{6}C$$ will have 8 neutrons, 6 protons, and 6 electrons.

p. 64.

```
     H   H   H   H   H
     |   |   |   |   |
 H - C - C - C - C - C - H
     |   |   |   |   |
     H   H   H   H   H
          pentane
```

```
     H   H   H   H   H   H
     |   |   |   |   |   |
 H - C - C - C - C - C - C - H
     |   |   |   |   |   |
     H   H   H   H   H   H
            hexane
```

```
     H   H   H   H   H   H   H
     |   |   |   |   |   |   |
 H - C - C - C - C - C - C - C - H
     |   |   |   |   |   |   |
     H   H   H   H   H   H   H
              heptane
```

```
     H   H   H   H   H   H   H   H
     |   |   |   |   |   |   |   |
 H - C - C - C - C - C - C - C - C - H
     |   |   |   |   |   |   |   |
     H   H   H   H   H   H   H   H
                octane
```

```
     H   H   H   H   H   H   H   H   H
     |   |   |   |   |   |   |   |   |
 H - C - C - C - C - C - C - C - C - C - H
     |   |   |   |   |   |   |   |   |
     H   H   H   H   H   H   H   H   H
                  nonane
```

```
     H   H   H   H   H   H   H   H   H   H
     |   |   |   |   |   |   |   |   |   |
 H - C - C - C - C - C - C - C - C - C - C - H
     |   |   |   |   |   |   |   |   |   |
     H   H   H   H   H   H   H   H   H   H
                    decane
```

p. 68.   There will be 22 hydrogen atoms ($2 \times 10 + 2 = 22$).

p. 85.   Yes! There are 14 atoms on each side of the equation as shown below.

$$CH_3COO^- + H^+ + Na^+ + HCO_3^- \longrightarrow Na^+ + CH_3COO^- + CO_2 + H_2O$$

p. 88.   Cooking oil is less dense. It floats on water.

p. 126.   The black substance is carbon, which is found in all organic compounds.

Appendix

SCIENCE SUPPLY COMPANIES

Carolina Biological Supply Company
2700 York Road
Burlington, NC 27215-3398
(800) 334-5551
http://www.carolina.com

**Connecticut Valley Biological
Supply Company**
82 Valley Road
P.O. Box 326
Southampton, MA 01073
(800) 628-7748
http://www.ctvalleybio.com

Delta Education
80 Northwest Boulevard
P.O. Box 3000
Nashua, NH 03061-3000
(800) 258-1302
http://www.delta-education.com

Edmund Scientifics
60 Pearce Avenue
Tonawanda, NY 14150-6711
(800) 728-6999
http://scientificsonline.com

Educational Innovations, Inc.
362 Main Avenue
Norwalk, CT 06851
(888) 912-7474
http://www.teachersource.com

Fisher Science Education
4500 Turnberry Drive
Hanover Park, IL 60133
(800) 955-1177
http://www.fisheredu.com

Frey Scientific
80 Northwest Boulevard
Nashua, NH 03063
(800) 225-3739
http://www.freyscientific.com/

NASCO-Fort Atkinson
901 Janesville Avenue
P.O. Box 901
Fort Atkinson, WI 53538-0901
(800) 558-9595
http://www.nascofa.com/

NASCO-Modesto
4825 Stoddard Road
P.O. Box 3837
Modesto, CA 95352-3837
(800) 558-9595
http://www.enasco.com

Sargent-Welch
P.O. Box 4130
Buffalo, NY 14217
(800) 727-4368
http://www.sargentwelch.com

Science Kit & Boreal Laboratories
777 East Park Drive
P.O. Box 5003
Tonawanda, NY 14151-5003
(800) 828-7777
http://sciencekit.com

Ward's Natural Science
P.O. Box 92912
Rochester, NY 14692-9012
(800) 962-2660
http://www.wardsci.com

Further Reading

Brent, Lynnette. *Elements and Compounds.* New York: Crabtree Publishing Company, 2009.

Clowes, Martin. *Organic Chemistry, Vol. 8, Chemistry Matters!* Danbury, Conn.: Grolier, 2007.

Crocker, Betty. *Betty Crocker's Cookbook: Everything You Need to Know to Cook.* Foster City, Calif.: IDG Books Worldwide, 2000.

The Diagram Group. *Chemistry: An Illustrated Guide to Science.* New York: Facts On File, 2006.

Kobilinsky, Lewis, Louis Levine, and Henrietta Margolis-Nunno. *Forensic DNA Analysis.* New York: Chelsea House, 2007.

Newton, David E. *Food Chemistry.* New York: Facts On File, 2007.

Robertson, William C. *Chemistry Basics.* Arlington, Virginia: National Science Teachers Association, 2007.

Other books by Robert Gardner:

Gardner, Robert, Salvatore Tocci, and Kenneth G. Rainis. *Ace Your Chemistry Science Project: Great Science Fair Ideas.* Berkeley Heights, N.J.: Enslow Publishers, Inc., 2010.

Gardner, Robert. *Ace Your Science Project Using Chemistry Magic and Toys: Great Science Fair Ideas.* Berkeley Heights, N.J.: Enslow Publishers, Inc., 2010.

———. *Chemistry Projects with a Laboratory You Can Build.* Berkeley Heights, N.J.: Enslow Publishers, Inc., 2008.

———. *Easy Genius Science Projects with Chemistry: Great Experiments and Ideas.* Berkeley Heights, N.J.: Enslow Publishers, Inc., 2009.

Internet Addresses

Boston Museum of Science.
    <http://www.mos.org>

Chemistry for Kids.
    <http://www.chem4kids.com/>

The Exploratorium. Exploratorium Home Page.
    <http://www.exploratorium.edu>

Index